BENJAMIN HOFF

The Tao of Pooh

Illustrated by Ernest H. Shepard

Mandarin

A Mandarin Paperback

THE TAO OF POOH

First published in Great Britain 1982
by Methuen Children's Books Ltd
This edition published 1989
by Mandarin Paperbacks
Michelin House, 81 Fulham Road, London sw3 6RB
and Auckland, Melbourne, Singapore and Toronto

Reprinted 1989, 1990 (twice), 1991 (twice), 1992 (three times),
1993 (five times), 1994 (three times)

Copyright © Benjamin Hoff 1982

ISBN 0 7493 0179 1

A CIP catalogue record for this title
is available from the British Library

Printed and bound in Great Britain by
BPC Paperbacks Ltd
A member of
The British Printing Company Ltd

The Tao of Pooh

The Tao of Pooh

'"When you wake up in the morning, Pooh," said Piglet at last, "what's the first thing you say to yourself?"

"What's for breakfast?" said Pooh. "What do *you* say, Piglet?"

"I say, I wonder what's going to happen exciting *today*?" said Piglet.

Pooh nodded thoughtfully.
"It's the same thing," he said.

"What's that?" the Unbeliever asked.
"Wisdom from a Western Taoist," I said.'

If you'd never thought of Pooh Bear in quite this light before, read on ...

For Han Hsiang-tse

Cottleston, Cottleston, Cottleston Pie,
A fly can't bird, but a bird can fly.
Ask me a riddle and I reply:
"Cottleston, Cottleston, Cottleston Pie."

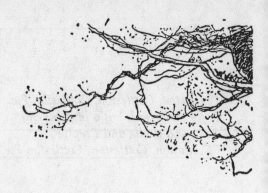

Contents

Foreword   xii

The *How* of Pooh?   1

The Tao of *Who?*   9

Spelling Tuesday   23

Cottleston Pie   37

The Pooh Way   67

Bisy Backson 91
That Sort of Bear 115
Nowhere and Nothing 141
The Now of Pooh 153
Backword 157

Foreword

"What's this you're writing?" asked Pooh, climbing onto the writing table.

"The Tao of Pooh," I replied.

"The *how* of Pooh?" asked Pooh, smudging one of the words I had just written.

"The *Tao* of Pooh," I replied, poking his paw away with my pencil.

"It seems more like the *ow!* of Pooh," said Pooh, rubbing his paw.

"Well, it's not," I replied huffily.

"What's it about?" asked Pooh, leaning forward and smearing another word.

"It's about how to stay happy and calm under all circumstances!" I yelled.

"Have you read it?" asked Pooh.

That was after some of us were discussing the Great Masters of Wisdom, and someone was saying how all of them came from the East, and I was saying that some of them didn't, but he was going on and on, just like this sentence, not paying any attention, when I decided to read a quotation of Wisdom from the West, to prove that there was more to the world than one half, and I read:

> "When you wake up in the morning, Pooh," said Piglet at last, "what's the first thing you say to yourself?"
>
> "What's for breakfast?" said Pooh. "What do *you* say, Piglet?"
>
> "I say, I wonder what's going to happen exciting *today?*" said Piglet.
>
> Pooh nodded thoughtfully.
>
> "It's the same thing," he said.

"What's that?" the Unbeliever asked.

"Wisdom from a Western Taoist," I said.

"It sounds like something from *Winnie-the-Pooh*," he said.

"It is," I said.

"That's not about Taoism," he said.

"Oh, yes it is," I said.

"No, it's not," he said.

"What do you think it's about?" I said.

"It's about this dumpy little bear that wanders around asking silly questions, making up songs, and going through all kinds of adventures, without ever accumulating any amount of intellectual knowledge or losing his simpleminded sort of happiness. *That's* what it's about," he said.

"Same thing," I said.

That was when I began to get an idea: to write a book that explained the principles of Taoism through Winnie-the-Pooh, and explained Winnie-the-Pooh through the principles of Taoism.

When informed of my intentions, the scholars exclaimed, "Pre*pos*terous!" and things like that. Others said it was the stupidest thing they'd ever heard, and that I must be dreaming. Some said it was a nice idea, but too difficult. "Just where would you even begin?" they asked. Well, an old Taoist saying puts it this way: "A thousand-mile journey starts with one step."

So I think that we will start at the beginning . . .

The *How* of Pooh?

"You see, Pooh," I said, "a lot of people don't seem to know what Taoism is . . . ."

"Yes?" said Pooh, blinking his eyes.

"So that's what this chapter is for—to explain things a bit."

"Oh, I see," said Pooh.

"And the easiest way to do that would be for us to go to China for a moment."

"*What?*" said Pooh, his eyes wide open in amazement. "Right now?"

"Of course. All we need to do is lean back, relax, and there we are."

"Oh, I see," said Pooh.

Let's imagine that we have walked down a

narrow street in a large Chinese city and have found a small shop that sells scrolls painted in the classic manner. We go inside and ask to be shown something allegorical—something humorous, perhaps, but with some sort of Timeless Meaning. The shopkeeper smiles. "I have just the thing," he tells us. "A copy of *The Vinegar Tasters!*" He leads us to a large table and unrolls the scroll, placing it down for us to examine. "Excuse me—I must attend to something for a moment," he says, and goes into the back of the shop, leaving us alone with the painting.

Although we can see that this is a fairly recent version, we know that the original was painted long ago; just when is uncertain. But by now, the theme of the painting is well known.

We see three men standing around a vat of vinegar. Each has dipped his finger into the vinegar and has tasted it. The expression on each man's face shows his individual reaction. Since the painting is allegorical, we are to understand that these are no ordinary vinegar tasters, but are instead representatives of the "Three Teachings" of China, and that the vinegar they are sampling represents the Essence of Life. The three masters are K'ung Fu-tse (Confucius), Buddha, and Lao-tse, author of the oldest existing book of Taoism. The first has a sour look on his face, the second wears a bitter expression, but the third man is smiling.

To K'ung Fu-tse (kung FOOdsuh), life seemed rather sour. He believed that the present was out of step with the past, and that the government of man on earth was out of harmony with the Way of Heaven, the government of the universe. Therefore, he emphasized reverence for the Ancestors, as well as for the ancient rituals and ceremonies in which the emperor, as the Son of Heaven, acted as intermediary between limitless heaven and limited earth. Under Confucianism, the use of precisely measured court music, prescribed steps, actions, and phrases all added up to an extremely complex system of rituals, each used for a particular purpose at a particular time. A saying was recorded about K'ung Fu-tse: "If the mat was not straight, the Master would not sit." This ought to give an indication of the extent to which things were carried out under Confucianism.

To Buddha, the second figure in the painting, life on earth was bitter, filled with attachments and desires that led to suffering. The world was seen as a setter of traps, a generator of illusions, a revolving wheel of pain for all creatures. In order to find peace, the Buddhist considered it necessary to transcend "the world of dust" and reach Nirvana, literally a state of "no wind." Although the essentially optimistic attitude of the Chinese altered Buddhism considerably after it was brought in from its native India, the devout Buddhist often saw the way to Nirvana interrupted all the same by the bitter wind of everyday existence.

To Lao-tse (LAOdsuh), the harmony that naturally existed between heaven and earth from the very beginning could be found by anyone at any time, but not by following the rules of the Confucianists. As he stated in his *Tao Te Ching* (DAO DEH JEENG), the "Tao Virtue Book," earth was in essence a reflection of heaven, run by the same laws—*not* by the laws of men. These laws affected not only the spinning of distant planets, but the activities of the birds in the forest and the fish in the sea. According to Lao-tse, the more man interfered with the natural balance produced and governed by the universal laws, the further away the harmony retreated into the distance. The more forcing, the more trouble. Whether heavy or light, wet or dry, fast or slow, everything had its own nature already within it, which could not be violated without causing difficulties. When abstract and arbitrary rules were imposed from the outside, struggle was inevitable. Only then did life become sour.

To Lao-tse, the world was not a setter of traps

but a teacher of valuable lessons. Its lessons needed to be learned, just as its laws needed to be followed; then all would go well. Rather than turn away from "the world of dust," Lao-tse advised others to "join the dust of the world." What he saw operating behind everything in heaven and earth he called *Tao* (DAO), "the Way." A basic principle of Lao-tse's teaching was that this Way of the Universe could not be adequately described in words, and that it would be insulting both to its unlimited power and to the intelligent human mind to attempt to do so. Still, its nature could be understood, and those who cared the most about it, and the life from which it was inseparable, understood it best.

Over the centuries Lao-tse's classic teachings were developed and divided into philosophical, monastic, and folk religious forms. All of these could be included under the general heading of Taoism. But the basic Taoism that we are concerned with here is simply a particular way of appreciating, learning from, and working with whatever happens in everyday life. From the Taoist point of view, the natural result of this harmonious way of living is happiness. You might say that happy serenity is the most noticeable characteristic of the Taoist personality, and a subtle sense of humor is apparent even in the most profound

Taoist writings, such as the twenty-five-hundred-year-old *Tao Te Ching*. In the writings of Taoism's second major writer, Chuang-tse (JUANGdsuh), quiet laughter seems to bubble up like water from a fountain.

"But what does that have to do with vinegar?" asked Pooh.

"I thought I had explained that," I said.

"I don't think so," said Pooh.

"Well, then, I'll explain it now."

"That's good," said Pooh.

In the painting, why is Lao-tse smiling? After all, that vinegar that represents life must certainly have an unpleasant taste, as the expressions on the faces of the other two men indicate. But, through working in harmony with life's circumstances, Taoist understanding changes what others may perceive as negative into something positive. From the Taoist point of view, sourness and bitterness come from the interfering and unappreciative mind. Life itself, when understood and utilized for what it is, is sweet. That is the message of *The Vinegar Tasters*.

"Sweet? You mean like honey?" asked Pooh.

"Well, maybe not *that* sweet," I said. "That would be overdoing it a bit."

"Are we still supposed to be in China?" Pooh asked cautiously.

"No, we're through explaining and now we're back at the writing table."

"Oh."

"Well, we're just in time for a little something," he added, wandering over to the kitchen cupboard.

The Tao of *Who*?

We were discussing the definition of wisdom late one night, and we were just about to fall asleep from it all when Pooh remarked that his understanding of Taoist principles had been passed down to him from certain Ancient Ancestors.

"Like who?" I asked.

"Like Pooh Tao-tse, the famous Chinese painter," Pooh said.

"That's *Wu* Tao-tse."

"Or how about Li Pooh, the famous Taoist poet?" Pooh asked cautiously.

"You mean Li *Po*," I said.

"Oh," said Pooh, looking down at his feet.

Then I thought of something. "That doesn't

really matter, anyway," I said, "because one of the most important principles of Taoism was named after you."

"Really?" Pooh asked, looking more hopeful.

"Of course—*P'u*, the Uncarved Block."

"I'd forgotten," said Pooh.

So here we are, about to try to explain *P'u*, the Uncarved Block. In the classic Taoist manner, we won't try too hard or explain too much, because that would only Confuse things, and because it would leave the impression that it was all only an intellectual idea that could be left on the intellectual level and ignored. Then you could say, "Well, this idea is all very nice, but what does it amount to?" So instead, we will try to *show* what it amounts to, in various ways.

P'u, by the way, is pronounced sort of like Pooh, but without so much *oo*—like the sound you make when blowing a fly off your arm on a hot summer day.

Before we bring our Resident Expert in for a few illuminating remarks, let's explain something.

The essence of the principle of the Uncarved Block is that things in their original simplicity contain their own natural power, power that is easily spoiled and lost when that simplicity is changed.

For the written character *P'u,* the typical Chinese dictionary will give a definition of "natural, simple, plain, honest." *P'u* is composed of two separate characters combined: the first, the "radical" or root-meaning one, is that for tree or wood; the second, the "phonetic" or sound-giving one, is the character for dense growth or thicket. So from "tree in a thicket" or "wood not cut" comes the meaning of "things in their natural state"—what is generally represented in English versions of Taoist writing as the "uncarved block."

This basic Taoist principle applies not only to *things* in their natural beauty and function, but to people as well. Or Bears. Which brings us to Pooh, the very Epitome of the Uncarved Block. As an illustration of the principle, he may appear a bit *too* simple at times . . .

"I *think* it's more to the right," said Piglet nervously. "What do *you* think, Pooh?"

Pooh looked at his two paws. He knew that one of them was the right, and he knew that when you had decided which one of them was the right, then the other one was the left, but he never could remember how to begin.

"Well," he said slowly——

... but, no matter how he may seem to others, especially to those fooled by appearances, Pooh, the Uncarved Block, is able to accomplish what he does because he *is* simpleminded. As any old Taoist walking out of the woods can tell you, simpleminded does not necessarily mean *stupid*. It's rather significant that the Taoist ideal is that of the still, calm, reflecting "mirror-mind" of the Uncarved Block, and it's rather significant that Pooh, rather than the thinkers Rabbit, Owl, or Eeyore, is the true hero of *Winnie-the-Pooh* and *The House at Pooh Corner*:

"The fact is," said Rabbit, "we've missed our way somehow."

They were having a rest in a small sand-pit on the top of the Forest. Pooh was getting rather tired of that sand-pit, and suspected it of following them about, because whichever direction they started in, they always ended up at it, and each time, as it came through the mist at them, Rabbit said triumphantly, "Now I know where we are!" and Pooh said sadly, "So do I," and Piglet said nothing. He had tried to think of something to say, but the only thing he could think of was, "Help, help!" and it seemed silly to say that, when he had Pooh and Rabbit with him.

"Well," said Rabbit, after a long silence in which nobody thanked him for the nice walk they were having, "we'd better get on, I suppose. Which way shall we try?"

"How would it be," said Pooh slowly, "if, as soon as we're out of sight of this Pit, we try to find it again?"

"What's the good of that?" said Rabbit.

"Well," said Pooh, "we keep looking for Home and not finding it, so I thought that if we looked for this Pit, we'd be sure not to find it, which would be a Good Thing, because then we might find something that we *weren't* looking for, which might be just what we *were* looking for, really."

"I don't see much sense in that," said Rabbit. . . .

"If I walked away from this Pit, and then walked back to it, of *course* I should find it."

"Well, I thought perhaps you wouldn't," said Pooh. "I just thought."

"Try," said Piglet suddenly. "We'll wait here for you."

Rabbit gave a laugh to show how silly Piglet was, and walked into the mist. After he had gone a hundred yards, he turned and walked back again . . . and after Pooh and Piglet had waited twenty minutes for him, Pooh got up.

"I just thought," said Pooh. "Now then, Piglet, let's go home."

"But, Pooh," cried Piglet, all excited, "do you know the way?"

"No," said Pooh. "But there are twelve pots of honey in my cupboard, and they've been calling to me for hours. I couldn't hear them properly before, because Rabbit *would* talk, but if nobody says anything except those twelve pots, I *think*, Piglet, I shall know where they're calling from. Come on."

They walked off together; and for a long time Piglet said nothing, so as not to interrupt the pots; and then suddenly he made a squeaky noise . . . and an oo-noise . . . because now he began to know where he was; but he still didn't dare to say so out loud, in case he wasn't. And just when he was getting so sure of himself that it didn't matter whether the pots went on calling or not, there was a shout in front of them, and out of the mist came Christopher Robin.

After all, if it were Cleverness that counted most, Rabbit would be Number One, instead of that Bear. But that's not the way things work.

"We've come to wish you a Very Happy Thursday," said Pooh, when he had gone in and out once or twice just to make sure that he *could* get out again.

"Why, what's going to happen on Thursday?" asked Rabbit, and when Pooh had explained, and Rabbit, whose life was made up of Important Things, said, "Oh, I thought you'd really come about something," they sat down for a little . . . and by-and-by Pooh and Piglet went on again. The wind was behind them now, so they didn't have to shout.

"Rabbit's clever," said Pooh thoughtfully.

"Yes," said Piglet, "Rabbit's clever."

"And he has Brain."

"Yes," said Piglet, "Rabbit has Brain."

There was a long silence.

"I suppose," said Pooh, "that that's why he never understands anything."

And if Clever Rabbit doesn't quite have what it takes, Abrasive Eeyore certainly doesn't either. Why not? Because of what we could call the Eeyore Attitude. You might say that while Rabbit's little routine is that of Knowledge for the sake of Being Clever, and while Owl's is that of Knowledge for the sake of Appearing Wise, Eeyore's is Knowledge for the sake of Complaining About Something. As anyone who doesn't have it can see, the Eeyore Attitude gets in the way of things like wisdom and happiness, and pretty much prevents any sort of real Accomplishment in life:

> Eeyore, the old grey Donkey, stood by the side of the stream, and looked at himself in the water.
>
> "Pathetic," he said. "That's what it is. Pathetic."
>
> He turned and walked slowly down the stream for twenty yards, splashed across it, and walked slowly back on the other side. Then he looked at himself in the water again.
>
> "As I thought," he said. "No better from *this* side. But nobody minds. Nobody cares. Pathetic, that's what it is."
>
> There was a crackling noise in the bracken behind him, and out came Pooh.
>
> "Good morning, Eeyore," said Pooh.
>
> "Good morning, Pooh Bear," said Eeyore gloomily. "If it *is* a good morning," he said. "Which I doubt," said he.
>
> "Why, what's the matter?"
>
> "Nothing, Pooh Bear, nothing. We can't all, and some of us don't. That's all there is to it."

It's not that the Eeyore Attitude is necessarily without a certain severe sort of humor . . .

"Hallo, Eeyore," they called out cheerfully.

"Ah!" said Eeyore. "Lost your way?"

"We just came to see you," said Piglet. "And to see how your house was. Look, Pooh, it's still standing!"

"I know," said Eeyore. "Very odd. Somebody ought to have come down and pushed it over."

"We wondered whether the wind would blow it down," said Pooh.

"Ah, that's why nobody's bothered, I suppose. I thought perhaps they'd forgotten."

. . . it's just that it's really not so awfully much *fun*. Not like a few other points of view we can think of. A little too complex or something. After all, what is it about *Pooh* that makes him so lovable?

"Well, to begin with——" said Pooh.

—Yes, well, to begin with, we have the principle of the Uncarved Block. After all, what is the most appealing thing about Pooh? What else but—

"Well, to begin with——"

—simplicity, the Simplicity of the Uncarved Block? And the nicest thing about that Simplicity is its useful wisdom, the what-is-there-to-eat variety—wisdom you can get at.

Considering that, let's have *Pooh* describe the nature of the Uncarved Block.

"All right, Pooh, what can you tell us about the Uncarved Block?"

"The *what?*" asked Pooh, sitting up suddenly and opening his eyes.

"The Uncarved Block. *You* know . . ."

"Oh, the. . . . Oh."

"What do you have to say about it?"

"I didn't do it," said Pooh.

"You——"

"It must have been Piglet," he said.

"I did not!" squeaked Piglet.

"Oh, Piglet. Where did *you*——"

"I *didn't,*" Piglet said.

"Well, then, it was probably Rabbit," said Pooh.

"It wasn't *me!*" Piglet insisted.

"Did someone call?" said Rabbit, popping up from behind a chair.

"Oh—Rabbit," I said. "We're talking about the Uncarved Block."

"Haven't seen it," said Rabbit, "but I'll go ask Owl."

"That won't be nec——," I began.

"Too late now," said Pooh. "He's gone."

"I never even *heard* of the Uncarved Block," said Piglet.

"Neither did I," said Pooh, rubbing his ear.

"It's just a figure of speech," I said.

"A what of a *who?*" asked Pooh.

"A figure of speech. It means that, well, the Uncarved Block is a way of saying, 'like Pooh.' "

"Oh, is *that* all?" said Piglet.

"I wondered," said Pooh.

Pooh can't describe the Uncarved Block to us in words; he just *is* it. *That's* the nature of the Uncarved Block.

"A perfect description. Thank you, Pooh."

"Not at all," said Pooh.

When you discard arrogance, complexity, and a few other things that get in the way, sooner or later you will discover that simple, childlike, and mysterious secret known to those of the Uncarved Block: Life is Fun.

Now one autumn morning when the wind had blown all the leaves off the trees in the night, and was trying to blow the branches off, Pooh and Piglet were sitting in the Thoughtful Spot and wondering.

"What *I* think," said Pooh, "is I think we'll go to Pooh Corner and see Eeyore, because perhaps his house has been blown down, and perhaps he'd like us to build it again."

"What *I* think," said Piglet, "is I think we'll go and see Christopher Robin, only he won't be there, so we can't."

"Let's go and see *everybody*," said Pooh. "Because when you've been walking in the wind for miles, and you suddenly go into somebody's house, and he says, 'Hallo, Pooh, you're just in time for a little smackerel of something,' and you are, then it's what I call a Friendly Day."

Piglet thought that they ought to have a Reason for going to see everybody, like Looking for Small or Organizing an Expotition, if Pooh could think of something.

Pooh could.

"We'll go because it's Thursday," he said, "and we'll go to wish everybody a Very Happy Thursday. Come on, Pigiet."

From the state of the Uncarved Block comes the ability to enjoy the simple and the quiet, the natural and the plain. Along with that comes the ability to do things spontaneously and have them work, odd as that may appear to others at times. As Piglet put it in *Winnie-the-Pooh*, "Pooh hasn't much Brain, but he never comes to any harm. He does silly things and they turn out right."

To understand all this a little better, it might help to look at someone who is quite the opposite—someone like, well, say, *Owl* for example . . .

PLES RING
IF AN RNSR
IS REQRD

PLES CNOKE
IF AN RNSR
IS NOT REQD

Spelling Tuesday

Through copse and spinney marched Bear; down open slopes of gorse and heather, over rocky beds of streams, up steep banks of sandstone into the heather again; and so at last, tired and hungry, to the Hundred Acre Wood. For it was in the Hundred Acre Wood that Owl lived.

"And if anyone knows anything about anything," said Bear to himself, "it's Owl who knows something about something," he said, "or my name's not Winnie-the-Pooh," he said. "Which it is," he added. "So there you are."

So now we come to Owl's house, as some of us have so many times before, searching for answers to questions of one sort or another. Will we find the answers here?

Before we go in and take a look around, it seems appropriate to have a few Background Remarks about the kind of scholar that Owl represents, in relation to the attitudes and principles of Taoism that we are concerned with here.

To begin with, it is necessary to point out that in China, scholars were generally Confucianist in training and orientation, and therefore often spoke a somewhat different language from the Taoists, who tended to see Confucianist scholars as busy ants spoiling the picnic of life, rushing back and forth to pick up the bits and pieces dropped from above. In the final section of the *Tao Te Ching*, Lao-tse wrote, "The wise are not learned; the learned are not wise"—an attitude shared by countless Taoists before and since.

From the Taoist point of view, while the scholarly intellect may be useful for analyzing certain things, deeper and broader matters are beyond its limited reach. The Taoist writer Chuang-tse worded it this way:

> A well-frog cannot imagine the ocean, nor can a summer insect conceive of ice. How then can a scholar understand the Tao? He is restricted by his own learning.

(This and other selections from classic oriental texts are my own translations and adaptations.)

It seems rather odd, somehow, that Taoism, the way of the Whole Man, the True Man, the Spirit Man (to use a few Taoist terms), is for the most part interpreted here in the West by the Scholarly Owl—by the Brain, the Academician, the dry-as-dust Absentminded Professor. Far from reflecting the Taoist ideal of wholeness and independence, this incomplete and unbalanced creature divides all kinds of abstract things into little categories and compartments, while remaining rather helpless and disorganized in his daily life. Rather than learn from Taoist teachers and from direct experience, he learns intellectually and indirectly, from books. And since he doesn't usually put Taoist principles into practice in an everyday sort of way, his explanations of them tend to leave out some rather important details, such as how they work and where you can apply them.

On top of that, it is very hard to find any of the *spirit* of Taoism in the lifeless writings of the humorless Academic Mortician, whose bleached-out Scholarly Dissertations contain no more of the character of Taoist wisdom than does the typical wax museum.

But that is the sort of thing we can expect from the Abstract Owl, the dried-up Western descendant of the Confucianist Dedicated Scholar, who, unlike his Noble but rather Unimaginative ancestor, thinks he has some sort of monopoly on——

"What's *that?*" Pooh interrupted.

"What's *what?*" I asked.

"What you just said—the Confusionist, Desiccated Scholar."

"Well, let's see. The Confusionist, Desiccated Scholar is one who studies Knowledge for the sake of Knowledge, and who keeps what he learns to himself or to his own small group, writing pompous and pretentious papers that no one else can understand, rather than working for the enlightenment of others. How's that?"

"Much better," said Pooh.

"Owl is about to illustrate the Confusionist, Desiccated Scholar," I said.

"I see," said Pooh.

Which brings us back to Owl. Let's see—how did Rabbit describe the situation with Owl? Oh, here it is:

... you can't help respecting anybody who can spell TUESDAY, even if he doesn't spell it right; but spelling isn't everything. There are days when spelling Tuesday simply doesn't count.

"By the way, Pooh, how do *you* spell Tuesday?"

"Spell what?" asked Pooh.

"Tuesday. You know—Monday, Tuesday ..."

"My dear Pooh," said Owl, "*everybody* knows that it's spelled with a *Two.*"

"Is it?" asked Pooh.

"Of course," said Owl. "After all, it's the second day of the week."

"Oh, is *that* the way it works?" asked Pooh.

"All right, Owl," I said. "Then what comes after Twosday?"

"*Thirdsday,*" said Owl.

"Owl, you're just confusing things," I said. "This is the day after Tuesday, and it's not Thirds—I mean, *Thurs*day."

"Then what is it?" asked Owl.

"It's *Today!*" squeaked Piglet.

"My favorite day," said Pooh.

Ours, too. We wonder why the scholars don't think much of it. Perhaps it's because they Confuse themselves thinking about other days so much.

Now one rather annoying thing about scholars is that they are always using Big Words that some of us can't understand . . .

> "Well," said Owl, "the customary procedure in such cases is as follows."

> "What does Crustimoney Proseedcake mean?" said Pooh. "For I am a Bear of Very Little Brain, and long words Bother me."

> "It means the Thing to Do."

> "As long as it means that, I don't mind," said Pooh humbly.

. . . and one sometimes gets the impression that those intimidating words are there to *keep* us from understanding. That way, the scholars can appear Superior, and will not likely be suspected of Not Knowing Something. After all, from the scholarly point of view, it's practically a crime not to know everything.

But sometimes the knowledge of the scholar is a bit hard to understand because it doesn't seem to match up with our own experience of things. In other words, Knowledge and Experience do not necessarily speak the same language. But isn't the knowledge that comes from experience more valuable than the knowledge that doesn't? It seems fairly obvious to some of us that a lot of scholars need to go outside and sniff around—walk through the grass, talk to the animals. That sort of thing.

"Lots of people talk to animals," said Pooh.
"Maybe, but . . ."
"Not very many *listen*, though," he said.
"That's the problem," he added.

In other words, you might say that there is more to Knowing than just being correct. As the mystical poet Han-shan wrote:

A scholar named Wang
Laughed at my poems.
The accents are wrong,
He said,
Too many beats;
The meter is poor,
The wording impulsive.

I laugh at his poems,
As he laughs at mine.
They read like
The words of a blind man
Describing the sun.

Quite often, struggling like a scholar over relatively unimportant matters can make one increasingly Confused. Pooh described the Confusionist's state of mind quite accurately:

On Monday, when the sun is hot,
I wonder to myself a lot:
"Now is it true, or is it not,
That what is which and which is what?"

On Tuesday, when it hails and snows,
The feeling on me grows and grows
That hardly anybody knows
If those are these or these are those.

On Wednesday, when the sky is blue,
And I have nothing else to do,
I sometimes wonder if it's true
That who is what and what is who.

On Thursday, when it starts to freeze,
And hoar-frost twinkles on the trees,
How very readily one sees
That these are whose—but whose are these?

On Friday——

Yes, whose *are* these, anyway? To the Desiccated Scholars, putting names on things is the most vital activity in the world. *Tree. Flower. Dog.* But don't ask them to prune the tree, plant the flower, or take care of the dog, unless you enjoy Unpleasant

Surprises. Living, growing things are beyond them, it seems.

Now, scholars can be very useful and necessary, in their own dull and unamusing way. They provide a lot of information. It's just that there is Something More, and that Something More is what life is really all about.

Oops. "Say, Pooh, have you seen my other pencil?"

"I saw Owl using it a little while ago," said Pooh.

"Oh, here it is. What's this? 'Aardvarks and Their Aberrations.'"

"Beg pardon?" said Pooh.

"'Aardvarks and Their Aberrations'—what Owl was writing about."

"Oh, were they?" said Pooh.

"Say, this pencil's all chewed up."

One more funny thing about Knowledge, that of the scholar, the scientist, or anyone else: it always wants to blame the mind of the Uncarved Block—what *it* calls Ignorance—for problems that it causes itself, either directly or indirectly, through its own limitations, nearsightedness, or neglect. For example, if you build your house where the wind can blow it over, then let it go to pieces while you worry about how to spell *Marmalade*, what is likely to happen? Of course. Anyone knows that. Yet when Owl's house falls down, what does he have to say about it?

> "Pooh," said Owl severely, "did *you* do that?"
>
> "No," said Pooh humbly. "I don't *think* so."
>
> "Then who did?"
>
> "I think it was the wind," said Piglet. "I think your house has blown down."
>
> "Oh, is that it? I thought it was Pooh."
>
> "No," said Pooh.

For the chapter's concluding word about Knowledge for the sake of Knowledge, let's recall an incident from *The House at Pooh Corner*. Eeyore was busy intimidating Piglet with something he'd made from three sticks . . .

"Do you know what A means, little Piglet?"

"No, Eeyore, I don't."

"It means Learning, it means Education, it means all the things that you and Pooh haven't got. That's what A means."

"Oh," said Piglet again. "I mean, does it?" he explained quickly.

"I'm telling you. People come and go in this Forest, and they say, 'It's only Eeyore, so it doesn't count.' They walk to and fro saying 'Ha ha!' But do they know anything about A? They don't. It's just three sticks to *them*. But to the Educated—mark this, little Piglet—to the Educated, not meaning Poohs and Piglets, it's a great and glorious A. Not," he added, "just something that anybody can come and *breathe* on."

Then Rabbit came along . . .

"There's just one thing I wanted to ask you, Eeyore. What happens to Christopher Robin in the mornings nowadays?"

"What's this that I'm looking at?" said Eeyore, still looking at it.

"Three sticks," said Rabbit promptly.

"You see?" said Eeyore to Piglet. He turned to Rabbit. "I will now answer your question," he said solemnly.

"Thank you," said Rabbit.

"What does Christopher Robin do in the mornings? He learns. He becomes Educated. He instigorates—I *think* that is the word he mentioned, but I may be referring to something else—he instigorates Knowledge. In my small way I also, if I have the word right, am—am doing what he does. That, for instance, is——"

"An A," said Rabbit, "but not a very good one. Well, I must get back and tell the others."

Eeyore looked at his sticks and then he looked at Piglet. . . .

"He *knew?* You mean this A thing is a thing *Rabbit* knew?"

"Yes, Eeyore. He's clever, Rabbit is."

"Clever!" said Eeyore scornfully, putting a foot heavily on his three sticks. "Education!" said Eeyore bitterly, jumping on his six sticks. "What *is* Learning?" asked Eeyore as he kicked his twelve sticks into the air. "A thing *Rabbit* knows! Ha!"

So there.

"I know something that Rabbit doesn't know," said Piglet.
"Oh? What's that?" I asked.
"Well, I can't remember what it's called, but——"

"Oh, yes. That's what's coming up next," I said.

"Oh, what *is* it called?" said Piglet, tapping his foot.

"Well, let's see . . ''

Cottleston Pie

Remember when Kanga and Roo came to the Forest? Immediately, Rabbit decided that he didn't like them, because they were Different. Then he began thinking of a way to make them leave. Fortunately for everyone, the plan failed, as Clever Plans do, sooner or later.

Cleverness, after all, has its limitations. Its mechanical judgments and clever remarks tend to prove inaccurate with passing time, because it doesn't look very deeply into things to begin with. As in Rabbit's case, it has to change its opinions later on because of what it didn't see when it was forming them. The thing that makes someone *truly* different—unique, in fact—is something that Cleverness cannot really understand.

We will refer to that special Something here as Inner Nature. Since it's pretty much beyond the power of the intellect to measure or understand, we will have *Pooh* explain it to us, which he will do by way of the Cottleston Pie Principle.

"Er . . . (cough). . . . A*hum*."

Excuse me a moment.

"Yes, Pooh?"

"*Me* explain it?" said Pooh behind his paw.

"Well, yes—I thought that might be nice."

"Why don't *you* explain it?" asked Pooh.

"Well, I thought it would be better if *you* did, somehow."

"I don't think that's such a good idea," said Pooh.

"Why not?"

"Because when I explain things, they get in the wrong places," he said. "That's why."

"All right, I'll explain it. But you can help out every now and then. How does that sound?"

"Much more like it," said Pooh.

Let's see. The Cottleston Pie Principle is based upon the song *Cottleston Pie*, which Pooh sang in *Winnie-the-Pooh*. Hmm . . .

"I say, Pooh. Maybe you'd better sing it again, in case anyone's forgotten."

"Certainly," said Pooh. "Now, let me see . . . (a*hem*),"

> *Cottleston, Cottleston, Cottleston Pie,*
> *A fly can't bird, but a bird can fly.*
> *Ask me a riddle and I reply:*
> *"Cottleston, Cottleston, Cottleston Pie."*

> *Cottleston, Cottleston, Cottleston Pie,*
> *A fish can't whistle and neither can I.*
> *Ask me a riddle and I reply:*
> *"Cottleston, Cottleston, Cottleston Pie."*

> *Cottleston, Cottleston, Cottleston Pie,*
> *Why does a chicken, I don't know why.*
> *Ask me a riddle and I reply:*
> *"Cottleston, Cottleston, Cottleston Pie."*

Now, let's start with——Ow! Oh, yes. "That was very nice, Pooh."

"Don't mention it."

Let's start with the first part: "A fly can't bird, but a bird can fly." Very simple. It's obvious, isn't it? And yet, you'd be surprised how many people violate this simple principle every day of their lives and try to fit square pegs into round holes, ignoring the clear reality that Things Are As They Are. We will let a selection from the writings of Chuang-tse illustrate:

> Hui-tse said to Chuang-tse, "I have a large tree which no carpenter can cut into lumber. Its branches and trunk are crooked and tough, covered with bumps and depressions. No builder would turn his head to look at it. Your teachings are the same—useless, without value. Therefore, no one pays attention to them."
>
> "As you know," Chuang-tse replied, "a cat is very skilled at capturing its prey. Crouching low, it can leap in any direction, pursuing whatever it is after. But when its attention is focused on such things, it can be easily caught with a net. On the other hand, a huge yak is not easily caught or overcome. It stands like a stone, or a cloud in the sky. But for all its strength, it cannot catch a mouse.
>
> "You complain that your tree is not valuable as lumber. But you could make use of the shade it provides, rest under its sheltering branches, and stroll beneath it, admiring its character and appearance. Since it would not be endangered by an axe, what could threaten its existence? It is useless to you only because you want to make it into something else and do not use it in its proper way."

In other words, everything has its own place and function. That applies to people, although many don't seem to realize it, stuck as they are in the wrong job, the wrong marriage, or the wrong house. When you know and respect your own Inner Nature, you know where you belong. You also know where you *don't* belong. One man's food is often another man's poison, and what is glamorous and exciting to some can be a dangerous trap to others. An incident in the life of Chuang-tse can serve as an example:

> While sitting on the banks of the P'u River, Chuang-tse was approached by two representatives of the Prince of Ch'u, who offered him a position at court. Chuang-tse watched the water flowing by as if he had not heard. Finally, he remarked, "I am told that the Prince has a sacred tortoise, over two thousand years old, which is kept in a box, wrapped in silk and brocade." "That is true," the officials replied. "If the tortoise had been given a choice," Chuang-tse continued, "which do you think he would have liked better—to have been alive in the mud, or dead within the palace?" "To have been alive in the mud, of course," the men answered. "I too prefer the mud," said Chuang-tse. "Good-bye."

"I like mud, too," said Pooh.

"Yes . . . well, anyway——"

"On a hot summer day? Nothing like it," he said.

"But the point is——"

"It keeps you cool," he said.

"That's not important here, Pooh," I said.

"It's *not?*" he asked in a shocked sort of way.

"I mean, there are other things to be——"

"How do you know?" said Pooh. "Have you ever tried it?"

"No, but——"

"Just the thing for a hot summer day," he continued, leaning back and closing his eyes. "Down by the river, covered with mud . . ."

"Look, Pooh——"

"Mud's nice," said Piglet, walking over to the writing table and looking up at us. "It adds color to your skin."

"Can't say *I* ever cared for it," said Owl, flying over and perching on the lamp. "It sticks in one's feathers. Rather disagreeable."

"You see?" I said. "Everyone's different. That's what we were discussing."

"I thought we were talking about mud," said Piglet.

"So did I," said Pooh.

"Well, I must get back to my encyclopedia," said Owl.

And now, if we can, let's go on to the second

part: "A fish can't whistle and neither can I." Coming from a wise mind, such a statement would mean, "I have certain limitations, and I know what they are." Such a mind would act accordingly. There's nothing wrong with not being able to whistle, especially if you're a fish. But there can be lots of things wrong with blindly trying to do what you aren't designed for. Fish don't live in trees, and birds don't spend too much time underwater if they can help it. Unfortunately, some *people*—who always seem to think they're smarter than fish and birds, somehow—aren't so wise, and end up causing big trouble for themselves and others.

That doesn't mean that we need to stop changing and improving. It just means that we need to recognize What's There. If you face the fact that you have weak muscles, say, then you can do the right things and eventually become strong. But if you ignore What's There and try to lift someone's car out of a ditch, what sort of condition will you be in after a while? And even if you have more muscle than anyone alive, you still can't push over a freight train. The wise know their limitations; the foolish do not.

To demonstrate what we mean, we can think of no one better than Tigger, who doesn't know his limitations.

Oh, excuse me. He says he does *now*.

Well, let's recall how he was forced to recognize *one* of them, anyway. Roo and Tigger were walking through the Forest one morning, and Tigger was talking about all the things that Tiggers can do . . .

"Can they fly?" asked Roo.

"Yes," said Tigger, "they're very good flyers, Tiggers are, Stornry good flyers."

"Oo!" said Roo. "Can they fly as well as Owl?"

"Yes," said Tigger. "Only they don't want to."

Well, after this sort of talk had gone on for a while, they arrived at the Six Pine Trees:

"I can swim," said Roo. "I fell into the river, and I swimmed. Can Tiggers swim?"

"Of course they can. Tiggers can do everything."

"Can they climb trees better than Pooh?" asked Roo, stopping under the tallest Pine Tree, and looking up at it.

"Climbing trees is what they do best," said Tigger. "Much better than Poohs."

And the next thing they knew, they were stuck in the tallest pine tree. Well, well. Not so good.

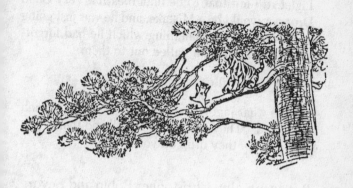

But then Pooh and Piglet came along, and of course Pooh realized right away just what was happening. Well, not *right* away ...

"It's a Jagular," he said.

"What do Jagulars do?" asked Piglet, hoping that they wouldn't.

"They hide in the branches of trees, and drop on you as you go underneath," said Pooh. "Christopher Robin told me."

"Perhaps we better hadn't go underneath, Pooh. In case he dropped and hurt himself."

"They don't hurt themselves," said Pooh. "They're such very good droppers."

Piglet still felt that to be underneath a Very Good
Dropper would be a Mistake, and he was just going
to hurry back for something which he had forgotten when the Jagular called out to them.

"Help! Help!" it called.

"That's what Jagulars always do," said Pooh, much
interested. "They call 'Help! Help!' and then when
you look up, they drop on you."

But eventually, Christopher Robin and Eeyore
came along, and a Rescue Net was formed. Then
Roo jumped and was Saved, and Tigger jumped
(sort of) . . .

. . . and was Saved (sort of):

There was a crash, and a tearing noise, and a confused heap of everybody on the ground.

Christopher Robin and Pooh and Piglet picked
themselves up first, and then they picked Tigger
up, and underneath everybody else was Eeyore.

"Quite a bit of trouble you put everyone
through, wasn't it, Tigger?"
"I learned from the experience, though," he
said, a bit evasively.
"Oh, did you?"

"Of course. You won't find me doing anything like *that* again," he said in a confident sort of way.

"That's good," I said. "On your way to somewhere, are you?"

"Yes," he said. "Roo and I are going swimming."

"Oh. Well, don't forget to take a rope."

"A rope? Why a rope?" said Tigger.

"Oh, just in case you see somebody fall in," I said.

"Now why didn't *I* think of that?" said Tigger.

A saying from the area of Chinese medicine would be appropriate to mention here: "One disease, long life; no disease, short life." In other words, those who know what's wrong with them and take care of themselves accordingly will tend to live a lot longer than those who consider themselves perfectly healthy and neglect their weaknesses. So, in that sense at least, a Weakness of some sort can do you a big favor, *if* you acknowledge that it's there. The same goes for one's limitations, whether Tiggers know it or not—and Tiggers usually don't. That's the trouble with Tiggers, you know: they can do *everything*. Very unhealthy.

Once you face and understand your limitations, you can work *with* them, instead of having them work against you and get in your way, which is what they do when you ignore them, whether you realize it or not. And then you will find that, in many cases, your limitations can be your strengths.

For example, when Owl's house fell down, who was able to escape, even though there was a heavy branch across the door and the only way out was through the letter-slot?

Piglet, the Very Small Animal.

Now, the last part of the principle: "Why does a chicken, I don't know why." Why does a chicken do what it does? You don't know? Neither do we. Neither does anyone else. Science likes to strut around and Act Smart by putting its labels on everything, but if you look at them closely, you'll see that they don't really say much. "Genes"? "DNA"? Just scratching the surface. "Instinct"? You know what *that* means:

CURIOUS: "Why do birds fly South for the winter?"
SCIENCE: "Instinct."

It means, "We don't know."

The important thing is, we don't really *need* to know. We don't need to imitate Nearsighted Science, which peers at the world through an electron microscope, looking for answers it will never find and coming up with more questions instead. We don't need to play Abstract Philosopher, asking unnecessary questions and coming up with meaningless answers. What we need to do is recognize Inner Nature and work with Things As They Are. When we don't, we get into trouble.

Pooh and Piglet found this out when they tried to catch a Heffalump. Not really knowing what Heffalumps like to eat, Piglet assumed that they would be attracted by acorns, and Pooh thought—

but first, you remember what a Heffalump is, don't you?

One day, when Christopher Robin and Winnie-the-Pooh and Piglet were all talking together, Christopher Robin finished the mouthful he was eating and said carelessly: "I saw a Heffalump today, Piglet."

"What was it doing?" asked Piglet.

"Just lumping along," said Christopher Robin. "I don't think it saw *me.*"

"I saw one once," said Piglet. "At least, I think I did," he said. "Only perhaps it wasn't."

"So did I," said Pooh, wondering what a Heffalump was like.

"You don't often see them," said Christopher Robin carelessly.

"Not now," said Piglet.

"Not at this time of year," said Pooh.

That's what a Heffalump is. So Pooh and Piglet decided to capture one. The plan started out well . . .

Pooh's first idea was that they should dig a Very Deep Pit, and then the Heffalump would come along and fall into the Pit, and——

"Why?" said Piglet.

"Why what?" said Pooh.

"Why would he fall in?"

Pooh rubbed his nose with his paw, and said that the Heffalump might be walking along, humming a little song, and looking up at the sky, wondering if it would rain, and so he wouldn't see the Very Deep Pit until he was half-way down, when it would be too late.

Piglet said that this was a very good Trap, but supposing it were raining already?

Pooh rubbed his nose again, and said that he hadn't thought of that. And then he brightened up, and said that, if it were raining already, the Heffalump would be looking at the sky wondering if it would *clear up*, and so he wouldn't see the Very Deep Pit until he was half-way down. . . . When it would be too late.

Piglet said that, now that this point had been explained, he thought it was a Cunning Trap.

Pooh was very proud when he heard this, and he felt that the Heffalump was as good as caught already, but there was just one other thing which had to be thought about, and it was this. *Where should they dig the Very Deep Pit?*

Piglet said that the best place would be somewhere where a Heffalump was, just before he fell into it, only about a foot farther on.

"But then he would see us digging it," said Pooh.

"Not if he was looking at the sky."

It sounds easy, doesn't it? Let's see. First, you dig a hole . . .

. . . making sure that it's big enough for a Heffa-lump.

And the best way to make sure that the Heffalump gets into the Trap once you've made it is to
put something that Heffalumps like into it, such as
a bag of peanuts, or——

"Honey," said Pooh.

"Honey?"

"A jar of honey," said Pooh.

"Are you sure?"

"A big jar of honey," Pooh insisted.

"Who ever heard of Heffalumps liking *honey?*
Sticky, gooey . . . How would they ever——"

"The best thing," said Pooh.

All right, *honey.* You put the honey in the
Trap, and before you know it, you've caught a . . .

Hmm. Something went wrong. That's not a Heffalump. But what is it? Maybe Piglet will find out when he goes to see what's in the Trap.

"Help, help!" cried Piglet, "a Heffalump, a Horrible Heffalump!" and he scampered off as hard as he could, still crying out, "Help, help, a Herrible Hoffalump! Hoff, Hoff, a Hellible Horralump! Holl, Holl, a Hoffable Hellerump!" And he didn't stop crying and scampering until he got to Christopher Robin's house.

"Whatever's the matter, Piglet?" said Christopher Robin who was just getting up.

"Heff," said Piglet, breathing so hard that he could hardly speak, "a Hell—a Heff—a Heffalump."

"Where?"

"Up there," said Piglet, waving his paw.

"What did it look like?"

"Like—like——It had the biggest head you ever saw, Christopher Robin. A great enormous thing, like—like nothing. A huge big—well, like a—I don't know—like an enormous big nothing. Like a jar."

So the honey wasn't such a good thing to use, after all. We didn't think that it really matched the Nature of Heffalumps, somehow.

Now that we know the principle, we can——

"Oh, it's you, Pooh."

"Mufflewuffle *Cottleston Pie* mufflewuffle."

"I beg your pardon?"

"Tell them about *Cottleston Pie*—what it means," Pooh whispered, a little more clearly.

"I just did," I said.

"I mean, tell them what it *stands* for," said Pooh expectantly.

"Oh, of course. Thank you, Pooh."

Pooh wants us to know that the words *Cottleston Pie* are a way of saying *Inner Nature*. So, by substituting that term for the last line in each verse of the song, we get:

Ask me a riddle and I reply:
"Inner Nature."

Hmm.

"*Cottleston Pie* sounds better," said Pooh.

"Well, how about this, Pooh?"

Ask me a riddle and I reply:
"Things Are As They Are."

"Better. . . . But it still doesn't rhyme."
"All right, how's *this?*"

Ask me a riddle and I reply:
"Cottleston, Cottleston, Cottleston Pie."

"Just right," said Pooh.

Now that we know the principle, we can look
at its applications. As we have likely recognized by
now, no two snowflakes, trees, or animals are alike.
No two *people* are the same, either. Everything has
its own Inner Nature. Unlike other forms of life,
though, people are easily led away from what's
right for them, because people have Brain, and
Brain can be fooled. Inner Nature, when relied on,
cannot be fooled. But many people do not look at it
or listen to it, and consequently do not understand
themselves very much. Having little understanding
of themselves, they have little respect for themselves, and are therefore easily influenced by others.

But, rather than be carried along by circumstances and manipulated by those who can see the
weaknesses and behavior tendencies that we ignore, we can work with our own characteristics and
be in control of our own lives. The Way of Self-Re-
liance starts with recognizing who we are, what
we've got to work with, and what works best for us.

"How would *you* explain it, Pooh?"

"With a song," he said. "A little something I just made up."

"Go ahead."

"Certainly . . . (cough)."

How can you get very far,
If you don't know Who You Are?
How can you do what you ought,
If you don't know What You've Got?
And if you don't know Which To Do
Of all the things in front of you,
Then what you'll have when you are through
Is just a mess without a clue
Of all the best that can come true
If you know What and Which and Who.

"That's it," he said, leaning back and closing his eyes.

"A Masterpiece."

"Well, better than average, maybe."

Sooner or later, we are bound to discover some things about ourselves that we don't like. But once we see they're there, we can decide what we want to do with them. Do we want to get rid of them completely, change them into other things, or use them in beneficial ways? The last two approaches are often especially Useful, since they avoid head-on conflict, and therefore minimize struggle. Also, they allow those transformed characteristics to be added to the list of things we have that help us out.

In a similar manner, instead of struggling to erase what are referred to as negative emotions, we can learn to use them in positive ways. We could describe the principle like this: while pounding on the piano keys may produce noise, removing them doesn't exactly further the creation of music. The principles of Music and Living aren't all that different, we think.

"Wouldn't you say, Pooh?"

"Say what?" asked Pooh, opening his eyes.

"Music and Living——"

"The same thing," said Pooh.

That's what we thought. So rather than work against ourselves, all we need to do in many cases is to point our weaknesses or unpleasant tendencies in a different direction than we have been.

The following incident recorded by the Taoist Liu An can serve to illustrate:

In the state of Ch'u, a housebreaker became a soldier under the General Tzu-fa, a man known for utilizing the abilities of others to a remarkable degree.

A short while later, Ch'u was attacked by the army of the state of Ch'i. Tzu-fa's men went out to counter the attack, but were driven back three times. The Ch'u strategists exhausted their minds while the enemy forces grew stronger.

At that point, the housebreaker stepped forward and asked for a chance to work for the defense of Ch'u. The General granted his request.

That night, the housebreaker sneaked into the Ch'i camp, entered the general's tent, and removed the curtains from the bed. Tzu-fa sent these back the next morning by special envoy, with a note which explained that they had been found by some men who were out gathering firewood.

The following evening, the housebreaker removed the Ch'i general's pillow. The next morning, it was returned with a message like the first.

On the third night, the housebreaker removed the general's jade hairpin. It was returned the next morning.

That day, the Ch'i general called his officers together. "One more night," he warned them, "and it will be my *head!*" The troops were ordered to break camp and return home.

So there is no such thing as an ability that is too useless, too crooked, or too small. It only depends on what you do with it. As Lao-tse pointed out, the bad can be raw material for the good.

So quite often, the easiest way to get rid of a Minus is to change it into a Plus. Sometimes you will find that characteristics you try hard to eliminate eventually come back, anyway. But if you do the right things, they will come back in the right ways. And sometimes those very tendencies that you dislike the most can show up in the right way at the right time to save your life, somehow. If that's ever happened to you, you'll think twice before setting out to completely Unbounce yourself.

What do we mean by Unbounce yourself? Well, you remember the situation with Tigger . . .

"How did you fall in, Eeyore?" asked Rabbit, as he dried him with Piglet's handkerchief.

"I didn't," said Eeyore.

"But how——"

"I was BOUNCED," said Eeyore.

"Oo," said Roo excitedly, "did somebody push you?"

"Somebody BOUNCED me. I was just thinking by the side of the river—thinking, if any of you know what that means, when I received a loud BOUNCE."

"Oh, Eeyore!" said everybody.

"Are you sure you didn't slip?" asked Rabbit wisely.

"Of course I slipped. If you're standing on the slippery bank of a river, and somebody BOUNCES you loudly from behind, you slip. What did you think I did?"

"But who did it?" asked Roo.

Eeyore didn't answer.

"I expect it was Tigger," said Piglet nervously.

"But, Eeyore," said Pooh, "was it a Joke, or an Accident? I mean——"

"I didn't stop to ask, Pooh. Even at the very bottom of the river I didn't stop to say to myself, 'Is this a Hearty Joke, or is it the Merest Accident?' I just floated to the surface, and said to myself, 'It's wet.' If you know what I mean."

So, to remove the Bounce from Tigger, Rabbit came up with another one of his famous plans: Rabbit, Pooh, and Piglet would take Tigger to somewhere at the top of the Forest where he'd never been, and lose him there. And from then on, he would be a Small and Sorry Tigger who bounced no more. Well, so much for Cleverness, as Eeyore might say, because as things turned out, Rabbit got *everyone* lost, including himself. Everyone but Tigger, that is. Tiggers don't get lost, it so happens, not even in the mist at the top of the Forest. And that proved to be very Useful.

Because, although Pooh and Piglet found their way back after a while ...

"Where's Rabbit?"

"I don't know," said Pooh.

"Oh—well, I expect Tigger will find him. He's sort of looking for you all."

"Well," said Pooh, "I've got to go home for something, and so has Piglet, because we haven't had it yet, and——"

"I'll come and watch you," said Christopher Robin.

So he went home with Pooh, and watched him for quite a long time ... and all the time he was watching, Tigger was tearing round the Forest making loud yapping noises for Rabbit. And at last a very Small and Sorry Rabbit heard him. And the Small and Sorry Rabbit rushed through the mist at the noise, and it suddenly turned into Tigger; a Friendly Tigger, a Grand Tigger, a Large and Helpful Tigger, a Tigger who bounced, if he bounced at all, in just the beautiful way a Tigger ought to bounce.

"Oh, Tigger, I *am* glad to see you," cried Rabbit.

In the story of the Ugly Duckling, when did the Ugly Duckling stop feeling Ugly? When he realized that he was a Swan. Each of us has something Special, a Swan of some sort, hidden inside somewhere. But until we recognize that it's there, what can we do but splash around, treading water? The Wise are Who They Are. They work with what they've got and do what they can do.

There are things about ourselves that we need to get rid of; there are things we need to change. But at the same time, we do not need to be too desperate, too ruthless, too combative. Along the way to usefulness and happiness, many of those things will change themselves, and the others can be worked on as we go. The first thing we need to do is recognize and trust our own Inner Nature, and not lose sight of it. For within the Ugly Duckling is the Swan, inside the Bouncy Tigger is the Rescuer who knows the Way, and in each of us is something Special, and that we need to keep.

> For a long time they looked at the river beneath them, saying nothing, and the river said nothing too, for it felt very quiet and peaceful on this summer afternoon.

> "Tigger is all right *really,*" said Piglet lazily.

> "Of course he is," said Christopher Robin.

> "Everybody is *really,*" said Pooh. "That's what *I* think," said Pooh. "But I don't suppose I'm right," he said.

> "Of course you are," said Christopher Robin.

The Pooh Way

By the time it came to the edge of the Forest the stream had grown up, so that it was almost a river, and, being grown-up, it did not run and jump and sparkle along as it used to do when it was younger, but moved more slowly. For it knew now where it was going, and it said to itself, "There is no hurry. We shall get there some day."

Now we come to what could be called the most characteristic element of Taoism-in-action. In Chinese, it is known as *Wu Wei*. It is also the most characteristic element of Pooh-in-action. In English, it is not known as much of anything in particular. We believe that it's time that someone noticed it and called it something, so we will call it **the** Pooh Way.

Literally, *Wu Wei* means "without doing, causing, or making." But practically speaking, it means without meddlesome, combative, or egotistical effort. It seems rather significant that the character *Wei* developed from the symbols for a clawing hand and a monkey, since the term *Wu Wei* means no going against the nature of things; no clever tampering; no Monkeying Around.

The efficiency of *Wu Wei* is like that of water flowing over and around the rocks in its path—not the mechanical, straight-line approach that usually ends up short-circuiting natural laws, but one that evolves from an inner sensitivity to the natural rhythm of things.

Let's take an example from the writings of Chuang-tse:

At the Gorge of Lü, the great waterfall plunges for thousands of feet, its spray visible for miles. In the churning waters below, no living creature can be seen.

One day, K'ung Fu-tse was standing at a distance from the pool's edge, when he saw an old man being tossed about in the turbulent water. He called to his disciples, and together they ran to rescue the victim. But by the time they reached the water, the old man had climbed out onto the bank and was walking along, singing to himself.

K'ung Fu-tse hurried up to him. "You would have to be a ghost to survive that," he said, "but you seem to be a man, instead. What secret power do you have?"

"Nothing special," the old man replied. "I began to learn while very young, and grew up practicing it. Now I am certain of success. I go down with the water and come up with the water. I follow it and forget myself. I survive because I don't struggle against the water's superior power. That's all."

When we learn to work with our own Inner Nature, and with the natural laws operating around us, we reach the level of *Wu Wei*. Then we work with the natural order of things and operate on the principle of minimal effort. Since the natural world follows that principle, it does not make mistakes. Mistakes are made—or imagined—by man, the creature with the overloaded Brain who separates himself from the supporting network of natural laws by interfering and trying too hard.

Not like Pooh, the most *effortless* Bear we've ever seen.

"Just how do you do it, Pooh?"
"Do what?" asked Pooh.
"Become so Effortless."

"I don't *do* much of anything," he said.

"But all those things of yours get done."

"They just sort of happen," he said.

"Wait a minute. That reminds me of something from the *Tao Te Ching*," I said, reaching for a book. "Here it is—chapter thirty-seven. Translated, it reads something like, 'Tao does not do, but nothing is not done.'"

"That sounds like a Riddle," said Pooh.

"It means that Tao doesn't force or interfere with things, but lets them work in their own way, to produce results naturally. Then whatever needs to be done is done."

"I see," said Pooh.

"In Chinese, the principle would be *Wei Wu Wei*—'Do Without Doing.' From *Wei Wu Wei* comes *Tzu Jan*, 'Self So.' That means that things happen by themselves, spontaneously."

"Oh, I see," said Pooh.

For a basic example of the Pooh Way, let's recall something that happened in *The House at Pooh Corner* when Pooh, Piglet, Rabbit, and Roo were playing Poohsticks. They'd dropped their sticks off the bridge into the river, and had gone to the other side to see whose stick would come out first.

And they'd been waiting quite a while when out floated . . .

Eeyore. *Eeyore?*

"I didn't know you were playing," said Roo.

"I'm not," said Eeyore.

"Eeyore, what *are* you doing there?" said Rabbit.

"I'll give you three guesses, Rabbit. Digging holes in the ground? Wrong. Leaping from branch to branch of a young oak-tree? Wrong. Waiting for somebody to help me out of the river? Right. Give Rabbit time, and he'll always get the answer."

Then Pooh got an idea. They could drop some stones into the river, the stones would make waves, and the waves would wash Eeyore over to the river bank. Rabbit thought it was a good idea. Eeyore didn't.

"Supposing we hit him by mistake?" said Piglet anxiously.

"Or supposing you missed him by mistake," said Eeyore. "Think of all the possibilities, Piglet, before you settle down to enjoy yourselves."

But Pooh had got the biggest stone he could carry, and was leaning over the bridge, holding it in his paws.

"I'm not throwing it, I'm dropping it, Eeyore," he explained. "And then I can't miss—I mean I can't hit you. *Could* you stop turning round for a moment, because it muddles me rather?"

"No," said Eeyore. "I *like* turning round."

Rabbit began to feel that it was time he took command.

"Now, Pooh," he said, "when I say 'Now!' you can drop it. Eeyore, when I say 'Now!' Pooh will drop his stone."

"Thank you very much, Rabbit, but I expect I shall know."

"Are you ready, Pooh? Piglet, give Pooh a little

more room. Get back a bit there, Roo. Are you ready?"

"No," said Eeyore.

"Now!" said Rabbit.

Pooh dropped his stone. There was a loud splash, and Eeyore disappeared. . . .

It was an anxious moment for the watchers on the bridge. They looked and looked . . . and even the sight of Piglet's stick coming out a little in front of Rabbit's didn't cheer them up as much as you would have expected. And then, just as Pooh was beginning to think that he must have chosen the wrong stone or the wrong river or the wrong day for his Idea, something grey showed for a moment by the river bank . . . and it got slowly bigger and bigger . . . and at last it was Eeyore coming out.

With a shout they rushed off the bridge, and pushed and pulled at him; and soon he was standing among them again on dry land.

"Oh, Eeyore, you *are* wet!" said Piglet, feeling him.

Eeyore shook himself, and asked somebody to explain to Piglet what happened when you had been inside a river for quite a long time.

"Well done, Pooh," said Rabbit kindly. "That was a good idea of ours."

Cleverness, as usual, takes all the credit it possibly can. But it's not the Clever Mind that's responsible when things work out. It's the mind that sees what's in front of it, and follows the nature of things.

When you work with *Wu Wei*, you put the round peg in the round hole and the square peg in the square hole. No stress, no struggle. Egotistical Desire tries to force the round peg into the square hole and the square peg into the round hole. Cleverness tries to devise craftier ways of making pegs fit where they don't belong. Knowledge tries to figure out why round pegs fit round holes, but not square holes. *Wu Wei* doesn't try. It doesn't think about it. It just does it. And when it does, it doesn't appear to do much of anything. But Things Get Done.

"Having trouble, Piglet?"

"The lid on this jar is *stuck*," gasped Piglet.

"Yes, it . . . *is*, isn't it. Here, Pooh, *you* open it."

(Pop.)

"Thanks, Pooh," said Piglet.

"Nothing, really," said Pooh.

"How did you get that lid off?" asked Tigger.

"It's easy," said Pooh. "You just twist on it like this, until you can't twist any harder. Then you take a deep breath and, as you let it out, *twist*. That's all."

"Let me try that!" yelled Tigger, bouncing into the kitchen. "Where's that new jar of pickles? Ah, here it is."

"Tigger," began Piglet nervously, "I don't think you'd better——"

"Nothing to it," said Tigger. "Just twist, and——"

CRASH!

"All right, Tigger," I said. "Get those pickles off the floor."

"Slipped out of my paw," explained Tigger.

"He tried too hard," said Pooh.

And when you try too hard, it doesn't work. Try grabbing something quickly and precisely with a tensed-up arm; then relax and try it again. Try doing something with a tense mind. The surest way to become Tense, Awkward, and Confused is to develop a mind that tries too hard—one that thinks too much. The animals in the Forest don't think too much; they just Are. But with an overwhelming number of people, to misquote an old Western philosopher, it's a case of "I think, therefore I am Confused." If you compare the City with the Forest, you may begin to wonder why it's *man* who goes around classifying himself as The Superior Animal.

"Superior to what?" asked Pooh.

"I don't know, Pooh. I've tried to think of *something*, but I just can't come up with an answer."

"If people were Superior to Animals, they'd take better care of the world," said Pooh.

"That's true," I said.

But down through the centuries, man has developed a mind that separates him from the world of reality, the world of natural laws. This mind tries too hard, wears itself out, and ends up weak and sloppy. Such a mind, even if of high intelligence, is inefficient. It goes here and there, backwards and forwards, and fails to concentrate on what it's doing at the moment. It drives down the street in a fast-moving car and thinks it's at the store, going over a grocery list. Then it wonders why accidents occur.

When you work with *Wu Wei*, you have no real accidents. Things may get a little Odd at times, but they work out. You don't have to try very hard to *make* them work out; you just *let* them. For example, let's recall the Search for Small. Small—which is short for Very Small Beetle, we were told—disappeared one day on his way around a gorse-bush. Nobody knew what happened.

So the Search was begun, and soon everyone was trying very hard to find Small. Everyone, of course, had been organized and directed by Rabbit. Everyone, of course, except for Pooh:

Bump!

"Ow!" squeaked something.

"That's funny," thought Pooh. "I said 'Ow!' without really oo'ing."

"Help!" said a small, high voice.

"That's me again," thought Pooh. "I've had an Accident, and fallen down a well, and my voice has gone all squeaky and works before I'm ready for it, because I've done something to myself inside. Bother!"

"Help—help!"

"There you are! I say things when I'm not trying. So it must be a very bad Accident." And then he thought that perhaps when he did try to say things he wouldn't be able to; so, to make sure, he said loudly: "A Very Bad Accident to Pooh Bear."

"Pooh!" squeaked the voice.

"It's Piglet!" cried Pooh eagerly. "Where are you?"

"Underneath," said Piglet in an underneath sort of way.

"Underneath what?"

Well, after *that* had been straightened out . . .

"Pooh!" he cried. "There's something climbing up your back."

"I thought there was," said Pooh.

"It's Small!" cried Piglet.

Those who do things by the Pooh Way find this sort of thing happening to them all the time. It's hard to explain, except by example, but it works. Things just happen in the right way, at the right time. At least they do when you *let* them, when you work *with* circumstances instead of saying, "This isn't supposed to be happening this way," and trying hard to make it happen some other way. If you're in tune with The Way Things Work, then they work the way they need to, no matter what you may think about it at the time. Later on, you can look back and say, "Oh, now I understand. That had to happen so that *those* could happen, and those had to happen in order for *this* to happen. . . ." Then you realize that even if you'd tried to make it all turn out perfectly, you couldn't have done better, and if you'd *really* tried, you would have made a mess of the whole thing.

Let's take another example of Things Work Out: Eeyore's birthday party, as arranged by Pooh and Piglet.

Pooh discovered, after Eeyore told him, that it was Eeyore's birthday. So Pooh decided to give him something. He went home to get a jar of honey to use as a birthday present, and talked things over with Piglet, who decided to give Eeyore a balloon that he'd saved from a party of his own. While Piglet went to get the balloon, Pooh walked off to Eeyore's with the jar of honey.

But after a while, he began to get Hungry.

So he sat down and took the top off his jar of honey. "Lucky I brought this with me," he thought. "Many a bear going out on a warm day like this would never have thought of bringing a little something with him." And he began to eat.

"Now let me see," he thought, as he took his last lick of the inside of the jar, "where was I going? Ah, yes, Eeyore." He got up slowly.

And then, suddenly, he remembered. He had eaten Eeyore's birthday present!

Well, most of it, anyway. Fortunately, he still had the *jar*. And since he was passing by the Hundred Acre Wood, he went in to see Owl and had him write *"A Happy Birthday"* on it. After all, it *was* a nice jar, even with nothing in it.

While all this was happening, Piglet had gone back to his own house to get Eeyore's balloon. He held it

very tightly against himself, so that it shouldn't
blow away, and he ran as fast as he could so as to

get to Eeyore before Pooh did; for he thought that
he would like to be the first one to give a present,
just as if he had thought of it without being told by
anybody. And running along, and thinking how
pleased Eeyore would be, he didn't look where he
was going . . . and suddenly he put his foot in a rabbit hole, and fell down flat on his face.

BANG!!!???°°°!!!

Yes, well, after Piglet fell on Eeyore's balloon,
it wasn't so . . . well, it was more . . . that is, it
was . . .

"Balloon?" said Eeyore. "You did say balloon? One of those big coloured things you blow up? Gaiety, song-and-dance, here we are and there we are?"

"Yes, but I'm afraid—I'm very sorry, Eeyore—but when I was running along to bring it to you, I fell down."

"Dear, dear, how unlucky! You ran too fast, I expect. You didn't hurt yourself, Little Piglet?"

"No, but I—I—oh, Eeyore, I burst the balloon!"

There was a very long silence.

"My balloon?" said Eeyore at last.

Piglet nodded.

"My birthday balloon?"

"Yes, Eeyore," said Piglet sniffing a little. "Here it is. With—with many happy returns of the day." And he gave Eeyore the small piece of damp rag.

"Is this it?" said Eeyore, a little surprised.

Piglet nodded.

"My present?"

Piglet nodded again.

"The balloon?"

And just then, Pooh arrived.

"I've brought you a little present," said Pooh excitedly.

"I've had it," said Eeyore.

Pooh had now splashed across the stream to Eeyore, and Piglet was sitting a little way off, his head in his paws, snuffling to himself.

"It's a Useful Pot," said Pooh. "Here it is. And it's got 'A Very Happy Birthday with love from Pooh' written on it. That's what all that writing is. And it's for putting things in. There!"

Then Eeyore discovered that, since the balloon was no longer as big as Piglet, it could easily be put away in the Useful Pot and taken out whenever it was needed, which certainly can't be done with the typical Unmanageable Balloon . . .

"I'm very glad," said Pooh happily, "that I thought of giving you a Useful Pot to put things in."

"I'm very glad," said Piglet happily, "that I thought of giving you Something to put in a Useful Pot."

But Eeyore wasn't listening. He was taking the balloon out, and putting it back again, as happy as could be. . . .

So it all worked out.

At its highest level, *Wu Wei* is indefinable and practically invisible, because it has become a reflex action. In the words of Chuang-tse, the mind of *Wu Wei* "flows like water, reflects like a mirror, and responds like an echo."

Just like Pooh. "*Ahem.* I say, *'Just like Pooh.'* "

"Wh—what?" said Pooh, waking up suddenly and falling out of the chair. "What's like who?"

"What flows like water, reflects like a mirror, and responds like an echo?"

"Oh, a Riddle," said Pooh. "How many guesses do I get?"

"Oh, I don't know. Let's just see what happens."

"What could it be?" he mumbled. "Flows like water . . ."

Using *Wu Wei*, you go by circumstances and listen to your own intuition. "This isn't the best time to do this. I'd better go *that* way." Like that. When you do that sort of thing, people may say you have a Sixth Sense or something. All it really is, though, is being Sensitive to Circumstances. That's just natural. It's only strange when you *don't* listen.

One of the most convenient things about this Sensitivity to Circumstances is that you don't have to make so many difficult decisions. Instead, you can let them make themselves.

For example, in *The House at Pooh Corner*, Pooh was wandering around one day trying to decide whom he wanted to visit. He could go see Eeyore, whom he hadn't seen since yesterday, or Owl, whom he hadn't seen since the day before yesterday, or Kanga, Roo, and Tigger, all of whom he hadn't seen for quite a while. How did he decide? He sat down on a rock in the middle of the stream and sang a song.

Then he got up and wandered around again, thinking about visiting Rabbit, until he found himself at his own front door. He went inside, got something to eat, and then went out to see Piglet.

That's how it is when you use the Pooh Way. Nothing to it. No stress, no mess. Now——

"A stream?" asked Pooh.

"What?"

"The answer. A *stream* flows like water, reflects like a mirror——"

"But it doesn't respond like an echo," I said.

"Yes, it does," said Pooh.

"Well, you're *close*. Sort of. I guess."

"Just give me more time," said Pooh.

The *Wu Wei* approach to conflict-solving can be seen in the practice of the Taoist martial art *T'ai Chi Ch'üan*, the basic idea of which is to wear the opponent out either by sending his energy back at him or by deflecting it away, in order to weaken his power, balance, and position-for-defense. Never is force opposed with force; instead, it is overcome with yielding.

"Flows like water, reflects like a mirror...," said Pooh, walking by.

"You're thinking too much, Pooh," I said. "I'll give you a hint; maybe it'll help."

"I hope so," said Pooh. "This is beginning to Bother me."

"All right—to solve the Riddle, you need to let your mind *flow* along and *reflect* what it sees. Then it can *respond* with the answer. Get it?"

"No," said Pooh.

"Oh, well."

"Let me see—flows like water. . . ," muttered Pooh.

The *Wu Wei* principle underlying *T'ai Chi Ch'üan* can be understood by striking at a piece of cork floating in water. The harder you hit it, the more it yields; the more it yields, the harder it bounces back. Without expending energy, the cork can easily wear you out. So, *Wu Wei* overcomes force by neutralizing its power, rather than by adding to the conflict. With other approaches, you may fight fire with fire, but with *Wu Wei*, you fight fire with water.

"*I* know," said Pooh. "A piece of cork!"

"What about it?"

"Responds like an echo!" he said triumphantly.

"But it doesn't flow like water or reflect like a mirror," I said.

"Oh," said Pooh. "That's right."

"Well, I guess I'd better tell you," I said. "It's the Pooh Way."

"What is?" asked Pooh.

"The answer," I said.

"Oh," said Pooh.

"That wasn't a very good Riddle," he added.

"All right, then *you* ask one."

"Glad to. What's black and white and red all over?"

"Oh, no. Not *that* one."

"You've heard it before?" asked Pooh, a bit surprised.

"Of course. It's been around for years. Everyone knows the answer—It's a newspaper."

"No," said Pooh.

"An embarrassed zebra?"

"No."

"Well, then . . ."

"Give up?" Pooh asked hopefully.

"All right, I give up. What's black and white and red all over?"

"A sunburned penguin."

"Pooh, that's stupid."

"Better than yours," he said.

"Well, here's another one, then. It has to do with the opposite of the Pooh Way. What runs around all day without getting anywhere?"

"A Rabbit?" said Pooh.

"Well, *practically*."

"Oh, I know. It's a——"

But we're saving *that* for the next chapter.

Bisy Backson

Rabbit hurried on by the edge of the Hundred Acre Wood, feeling more important every minute, and soon he came to the tree where Christopher Robin lived. He knocked at the door, and he called out once or twice, and then he walked back a little way and put his paw up to keep the sun out, and called to the top of the tree, and then he turned all round and shouted "Hallo!" and "I say!" "It's Rabbit!"— but nothing happened. Then he stopped and listened, and everything stopped and listened with him, and the Forest was very lone and still and peaceful in the sunshine, until suddenly a hundred miles above him a lark began to sing.

"Bother!" said Rabbit. "He's gone out."

He went back to the green front door, just to make sure, and he was turning away, feeling that his

morning had got all spoilt, when he saw a piece of
paper on the ground. And there was a pin in it, as if
it had fallen off the door.

"Ha!" said Rabbit, feeling quite happy again. "Another notice!"

This is what it said:

> GON OUT
> BACKSON
> BISY
> BACKSON.
>   C. R.

Rabbit didn't know what a Backson was—in
spite of the fact that he is one—so he went to ask
Owl. Owl didn't know, either. But we think *we*
know, and we think a lot of other people do, too.
Chuang-tse described one quite accurately:

There was a man who disliked seeing his footprints
and his shadow. He decided to escape from them,
and began to run. But as he ran along, more footprints appeared, while his shadow easily kept up
with him. Thinking he was going too slowly, he ran
faster and faster without stopping, until he finally
collapsed from exhaustion and died.

If he had stood still, there would have been no footprints. If he had rested in the shade, his shadow would have disappeared.

You see them almost everywhere you go, it seems. On practically any sunny sort of day, you can see the Backsons stampeding through the park, making all kinds of loud Breathing Noises. Perhaps you are enjoying a picnic on the grass when you suddenly look up to find that one or two of them just ran over your lunch.

Generally, though, you are safe around trees and grass, as Backsons tend to avoid them. They prefer instead to struggle along on asphalt and concrete, in imitation of the short-lived transportation machines for which those hard surfaces were designed. Inhaling poisonous exhaust fumes from the vehicles that swerve to avoid hitting them, the Backsons blabber away to each other about how much better they feel now that they have gone Outdoors. Natural living, they call it.

The Bisy Backson is almost desperately active. If you ask him what his Life Interests are, he will give you a list of Physical Activities, such as:

"Skydiving, tennis, jogging, racquet-ball, skiing, swimming, and water-skiing."

"Is that all?"

"Well, I (gasp, pant, wheeze) *think* so," says Backson.

"Have you ever tried chasing cars?"

"No, I—no, I never have."

"How about wrestling alligators?"

"No . . . I always wanted to, though."

"Roller-skating down a flight of stairs?"

"No, I never thought of it."

"But you said you were *active.*"

At this point, the Backson replies, thoughtfully, "I say—do you think there's something . . . *wrong* with me? Maybe I'm losing my energy."

After a while, maybe.

The Athletic sort of Backson—one of the many common varieties—is concerned with physical fitness, he says. But for some reason, he sees it as something that has to be pounded in from the outside, rather than built up from the inside. Therefore, he confuses exercise with *work.* He works when he works, works when he exercises, and, more often than not, works when he plays. Work, work, work. All work and no play makes Backson a dull boy. Kept up for long enough, it makes him dead, too.

Well—here's Rabbit. "Hello, Rabbit. What's new?"

"I just got back from Owl's," said Rabbit, slightly out of breath.

"Oh? You were certainly gone a long time."

"Yes, well ... Owl insisted on telling me a story about his Great-Uncle Philbert."

"Oh, *that's* why."

"But anyway—Owl said that he hasn't seen the Uncarved Block, either, but that Roo is probably playing with it. So I stopped off at Kanga's house, but no one was there."

"They're out in the Forest, practicing jumps with Tigger," I said.

"Oh. Well, I'd better be going, then."

"That's all right, Rabbit, because——"

Where'd he go? That's how it is, you know—no rest for the Backson.

Let's put it this way: if you want to be healthy, relaxed, and contented, just watch what a Bisy Backson does and then do the opposite. There's one now, pacing back and forth, jingling the loose coins in his pocket, nervously glancing at his watch. He makes you feel tired just looking at him. The chronic Backson always seems to have to be *going* somewhere, at least on a superficial, physical level. He doesn't go out for a *walk*, though; he doesn't have time.

"Not conversing," said Eeyore. "Not first one and then the other. You said 'Hallo' and Flashed Past. I saw your tail in the distance as I was meditating my reply. I *had* thought of saying 'What?'—but, of course, it was then too late."

"Well, I was in a hurry."

"No Give and Take," Eeyore went on. "No Exchange of Thought: *'Hallo—What'*——I mean, it gets you nowhere, particularly if the other person's tail is only just in sight for the second half of the conversation."

The Bisy Backson is always On The Run, it seems, always:

GONE OUT

BACK SOON

BUSY

BACK SOON

or, more accurately:

BACK OUT
GONE SOON
BUSY
GONE SOON

The Bisy Backson is always going *somewhere*, somewhere he hasn't been. Anywhere but where he is.

"That's just it," said Rabbit, "Where?"

"Perhaps he's looking for something."

"What?" asked Rabbit.

"That's just what I was going to say," said Pooh. And then he added, "Perhaps he's looking for a— for a——"

For a Reward, perhaps. Our Bisy Backson religions, sciences, and business ethics have tried their hardest to convince us that there is a Great Reward waiting for us somewhere, and that what we have to do is spend our lives working like lunatics to catch up with it. Whether it's up in the sky, behind the next molecule, or in the executive suite, it's somehow always farther along than we are—just down the road, on the other side of the world, past the moon, beyond the stars. . . .

"Ouch!" said Pooh, landing on the floor.

"That's what happens when you go to sleep on the edge of the writing table," I said. "You fall off."

"Just as well," said Pooh.

"Why's that?" I asked.

"I was having an awful dream," he said.

"Oh?"

"Yes. I'd found a jar of honey. . . ," he said, rubbing his eyes.

"What's awful about that?" I asked.

"It kept moving," said Pooh. "They're not supposed to do that. They're *supposed* to sit still."

"Yes, I know."

"But whenever I reached for it, this jar of honey would sort of go somewhere else."

"A nightmare," I said.

"Lots of people have dreams like that," I added reassuringly.

"Oh," said Pooh. "About Unreachable jars of honey?"

"About the same sort of thing," I said. "That's not unusual. The odd thing, though, is that some people *live* like that."

"Why?" asked Pooh.

"I don't know," I said. "I suppose because it gives them Something to Do."

"It doesn't sound like much fun to me," said Pooh.

No, it doesn't. A way of life that keeps saying, "Around the next corner, above the next step," works against the natural order of things and makes it so difficult to be happy and good that only a few get to where they would naturally have been in the first place—Happy and Good—and the rest give up and fall by the side of the road, cursing the world, which is not to blame but which is there to help show the way.

Those who think that the rewarding things in life are somewhere beyond the rainbow——

"Burn their toast a lot," said Pooh.

"I beg your pardon?"

"They burn their toast a lot," said Pooh.

"They—well, yes. And not only that——"

"Here comes Rabbit," said Pooh.

"Oh, there you are," said Rabbit.

"Here we are," said Pooh.

"Yes, here we are," I said.

"And there *you* are," said Pooh.

"Yes, here I am," said Rabbit impatiently. "To come to the point—Roo showed me his set of blocks. They're all carved and painted, with letters on them."

"Oh?" I said.

"Just the sort of thing you'd *expect* to see, actually," said Rabbit, stroking his whiskers thoughtfully. "So by process of elimination," he said, "that means *Eeyore* has it."

"But Rabbit," I said. "You see——"

"Yes," said Rabbit. "I see Eeyore and find out what he knows about it—that's clearly the next step."

"There he goes," said Pooh.

Looking back a few years, we see that the first Bisy Backsons in this part of the world, the Puritans, practically worked themselves to death in the fields without getting much of anything in return for their tremendous efforts. They were actually starving until the wiser inhabitants of the land showed them a few things about working in harmony with the earth's rhythms. Now you plant; now you relax. Now you work the soil; now you leave it alone. The Puritans never really understood the second half, never really believed in it. And so, after two or three centuries of pushing, pushing, and pushing the once-fertile earth, and a few years of depleting its energy still further with synthetic stimulants, we have apples that taste like cardboard, oranges that taste like tennis balls, and pears that taste like sweetened Styrofoam, all products of soil that is not allowed to relax. We're not supposed to complain, but There It Is.

"I say, Pooh, why aren't *you* busy?" I said.

"Because it's a nice day," said Pooh.

"Yes, but——"

"Why ruin it?" he said.

"But you could be doing something Important," I said.

"I am," said Pooh.

"Oh? Doing what?"

"Listening," he said.

"Listening to what?"

"To the birds. And that squirrel over there."

"What are they saying?" I asked.

"That it's a nice day," said Pooh.

"But you know that already," I said.

"Yes, but it's always good to hear that somebody else thinks so, too," he replied.

"Well, you could be spending your time getting Educated by listening to the Radio, instead," I said.

"That thing?"

"Certainly. How else will you know what's going on in the world?" I said.

"By going outside," said Pooh.

"Er . . . well. . . ." (Click.) "Now just listen to this, Pooh."

"Thirty thousand people were killed today when five jumbo airliners collided over downtown Los Angeles . . . ," the Radio announced.

"What does *that* tell you about the world?" asked Pooh.

"Hmm. You're right." (Click.)

"What are the birds saying now?" I asked.

"That it's a nice day," said Pooh.

It certainly is, even if the Backsons *are* too busy to enjoy it. But to conclude our explanation of why so busy . . .

The hardheaded followers of the previously mentioned Party-Crashing Busybody religion failed to appreciate the beauty of the endless forest and clear waters that appeared before them on the fresh green continent of the New World. Instead, they saw the paradise that was there and the people who lived in harmony with it as alien and threatening, something to attack and conquer—because it all stood in the way of the Great Reward. They didn't like singing very much, either. In fact——

"What?" said Pooh. "No singing?"

"Pooh, I'm trying to finish this. That's right, though. No singing. They didn't like it."

"Well, if they didn't like singing, then what was their attitude towards Bears?"

"I don't think they liked Bears, either."

"They didn't like *Bears?*"

"No. Not very much, anyway."

"No singing, no Bears. . . . Just what *did* they like?"

"I don't think they liked *anything,* Pooh."

"No wonder things are a little Confused around here," he said.

Anyway, from the Miserable Puritan came the Restless Pioneer, and from him, the Lonely Cowboy, always riding off into the sunset, looking for something just down the trail. From this rootless, dissatisfied ancestry has come the Bisy Backson, who, like his forefathers, has never really felt at home, at peace, with this Friendly Land. Rigid, combative fanatic that he is, the tightfisted Backson is just too hard on himself, too hard on others, and too hard on the world that heroically attempts to carry on in spite of what he is doing to it.

It's not surprising, therefore, that the Backson thinks of progress in terms of fighting and overcoming. One of his little idiosyncrasies, you might say. Of course, *real* progress involves growing and developing, which involves changing inside, but that's something the inflexible Backson is unwilling to do. The urge to grow and develop, present in all forms of life, becomes perverted in the Bisy Backson's mind into a constant struggle to change everything (the Bulldozer Backson) and everyone (the Bigoted Backson) else *but* himself, and interfere with things he has no business interfering with, including practically every form of life on earth. At least to a limited extent, his behavior has been held in check by wiser people around him. But, like parents of hyperactive children, the wise find that they can't be everywhere at once. Baby-sitting the Backsons wears you out.

"Here's Rabbit again," said Pooh. "And Eeyore."

"Oh—Rabbit," I said.

"*And* Eeyore," said Eeyore.

"I asked Eeyore——," said Rabbit.

"That's me," said Eeyore. "Eeyore."

"Yes, I remember," I said. "I saw you just last year, out in the Swamp somewhere."

"*Swamp?*" said Eeyore indignantly. "It's not a Swamp. It's a *Bog.*"

"Swamp, Bog. . . ."

"What's a Bog?" asked Pooh.

"If your ankles get wet, that's a Bog," said Eeyore.

"I see," said Pooh.

"Whereas," continued Eeyore, "if you sink in up to your *neck*, that's a Swamp."

"Swamp, indeed," he added bitterly. "Ha!"

"Anyway, I asked Eeyore," said Rabbit, "and he said he didn't have the slightest idea what I was talking about."

"It appears that I'm not alone in that," put in Eeyore. "You don't have the slightest idea, either. Obviously."

"Just what *is* the Uncarved Block?" asked Rabbit.

"It's me," said Pooh.

"*You?*" said Eeyore. "I came all the way over here——"

"From the Swamp," I added helpfully.

"—from the *Bog*, to see *Pooh?*"

"Why not?" asked Pooh.

"Anything for Rabbit to keep busy over," said Eeyore sarcastically. "Anything at all, apparently."

Now, one thing that seems rather odd to us is that the Bisy Backson Society, which practically worships youthful energy, appearance, and attitudes, has developed no effective methods of retaining them, a lack testified to by an ever-increasing reliance on the unnatural False Front approach of cosmetics and plastic surgery. Instead, it has developed countless ways of breaking youthfulness down and destroying it. Those damaging activities that are not part of the search for the Great Reward seem to accumulate under the general heading of Saving Time.

For an example of the latter, let's take a classic monument to the Bisy Backson: the Hamburger Stand.

In China, there is the Teahouse. In France, there is the Sidewalk Café. Practically every civilized country in the world has some sort of equivalent—a place where people can go to eat, relax, and talk things over without worrying about what time it is, and without having to leave as soon as the food is eaten. In China, for example, the Teahouse is a real social institution. Throughout the day, families, neighbors, and friends drop in for tea and light food. They stay as long as they like. Discussions may last for hours. It would be a bit strange to call the Teahouse the nonexclusive neighborhood social club; such terms are too Western. But that can roughly describe part of the function, at least from our rather compartmentalized point of view. "You're important. Relax and enjoy yourself." That's the message of the Teahouse.

What's the message of the Hamburger Stand? Quite obviously, it's: "You don't count; hurry up."

Not only that, but as everyone knows by now, the horrible Hamburger Stand is an insult to the customer's health as well. Unfortunately, this is not the only example supported by the Saving Time mentality. We could also list the Supermarket, the Microwave Oven, the Nuclear Power Plant, the Poisonous Chemicals. . . .

Practically speaking, if timesaving devices really saved time, there would be more time available to us now than ever before in history. But, strangely enough, we seem to have less time than even a few years ago. It's really great fun to go somewhere where there are no timesaving devices because, when you do, you find that you have *lots of time.* Elsewhere, you're too busy working to pay for machines to save you time so you won't have to work so hard.

The main problem with this great obsession for Saving Time is very simple: you can't *save* time. You can only spend it. But you can spend it wisely or foolishly. The Bisy Backson has practically no time at all, because he's too busy wasting it by trying to save it. And by trying to save every bit of it, he ends up wasting the whole thing.

Henry David Thoreau put it this way, in *Walden:*

> Why should we live with such hurry and waste of life? We are determined to be starved before we are hungry. Men say that a stitch in time saves nine, and so they take a thousand stitches to-day to save nine tomorrow.

For colorful contrast with the youth-destroying Bisy Backson Society, let's get back to Taoism for a moment. One of the most intriguing things about Taoism is that it not only contains respect for the old and wise, but also for the figure known as the Youthful Immortal. The Taoist tradition is filled with fascinating stories (fiction) and accounts (fact, embellished or otherwise) of those who, while still young, discovered the Secrets of Life. However the discoveries were made, the result in each case was the same: a long life of youthful appearance, outlook, and energy.

For that matter, Taoist Immortals of all age levels have traditionally been known for their young attitudes, appearances, and energies. These were hardly accidental, but resulted from Taoist practices. For centuries in China, the general life expectancy was not much more than forty years, and hardworking farmers and dissipated aristocrats often died even younger than that. Yet countless Taoists lived into their eighties and nineties, and many lived considerably longer. The following is one of our favorite examples.

In 1933, newspapers around the world announced the death of a man named Li Chung Yun. As officially and irrefutably recorded by the Chinese government, and as verified by a thorough independent investigation, Li had been born in 1677. When over the age of two hundred, he had given a series of twenty-eight, three-hour-long talks on longevity at a Chinese university. Those who saw him at that time claimed that he looked like a man in his fifties, standing straight and tall, with strong teeth and a full head of hair. When he died, he was two hundred fifty-six years old.

When Li was a child, he left home to follow some wandering herbalists. In the mountains of China, he learned from them some of the secrets of the earth's medicine. In addition to using various rejuvenative herbs daily, he practiced Taoist exercises, believing that exercise which strains and tires the mind and body shortens life. His favorite way of traveling was what he called "walking lightly." Young men who went for walks with him when he was in his later years could not match his pace, which he maintained for miles. He advised those who wanted strong health to "sit like a turtle, walk like a pigeon, and sleep like a dog." When asked for his major secret, though, he would reply, "inner quiet."

Speaking of that sort of thing, let's return to *The House at Pooh Corner.* Christopher Robin has just asked Pooh a question:

"What do you like doing best in the world, Pooh?"

"Well," said Pooh, "what I like best——" and then he had to stop and think. Because although Eating Honey *was* a very good thing to do, there was a moment just before you began to eat it which was better than when you were, but he didn't know what it was called.

The honey doesn't taste so good once it is being eaten; the goal doesn't mean so much once it is reached; the reward is not so rewarding once it has been given. If we add up all the rewards in our lives, we won't have very much. But if we add up the spaces *between* the rewards, we'll come up with quite a bit. And if we add up the rewards *and* the spaces, then we'll have everything—every minute of the time that we spent. What if we could enjoy it?

The Christmas presents once opened are Not So Much Fun as they were while we were in the process of examining, lifting, shaking, thinking about, and opening them. Three hundred sixty-five days later, we try again and find that the same thing has happened. Each time the goal is reached, it becomes Not So Much Fun, and we're off to reach the next one, then the next one, then the next.

That doesn't mean that the goals we have don't count. They do, mostly because they cause us to go through the process, and it's the *process* that makes us wise, happy, or whatever. If we do things in the wrong sort of way, it makes us miserable, angry, confused, and things like that. The goal has to be right for us, and it has to be beneficial, in order to ensure a beneficial process. But aside from that, it's really the process that's important. *Enjoyment* of the process is the secret that erases the myths of the Great Reward and Saving Time. Perhaps this can help to explain the everyday significance of the word *Tao*, the Way.

What could we call that moment before we begin to eat the honey? Some would call it anticipation, but we think it's more than that. We would call it awareness. It's when we become happy and realize it, if only for an instant. By Enjoying the Process, we can stretch that awareness out so that it's no longer only a moment, but covers the whole thing. Then we can have a lot of fun. Just like Pooh.

> And then he thought that being with Christopher Robin was a very good thing to do, and having Piglet near was a very friendly thing to have; and so, when he had thought it all out, he said, "What I like best in the whole world is Me and Piglet going to see You, and You saying 'What about a little something?' and Me saying, 'Well, I shouldn't mind a little something, should you, Piglet,' and it being a hummy sort of day outside, and birds singing."

When we take the time to enjoy our surroundings and appreciate being alive, we find that we have no time to be Bisy Backsons anymore. But that's all right, because being Bisy Backsons is a tremendous waste of time. As the poet Lu Yu wrote:

The clouds above us join and separate,
The breeze in the courtyard leaves and returns.
Life is like that, so why not relax?
Who can stop us from celebrating?

That Sort of Bear

We were discussing the "Ode to Joy," the choral finale to Beethoven's Ninth Symphony.

"It's one of my favorites," said Pooh.

"Same here," I said.

"My favorite part," said Pooh, "is where they go:

Sing Ho! for the life of a Bear!"

"But——"

"*Sing Ho! for a Bear!*
Sing Ho! for a Pooh!"

"But they don't——"

"Sing Ho! for the life of a Bear!"

"My favorite part," he added.

"But they don't *sing,* 'Sing Ho! for the life of a Bear!' in the 'Ode to Joy,' " I said.

"They don't?"

"No, they don't."

"Why not?"

"Well, because they hadn't *thought* of it, I guess."

"They *what?*"

"Neither Ludwig van Beethoven nor the man who wrote the words of the 'Ode to Joy' put anything in it about Bears."

"Oh. I must have been thinking of Ludwig van *Bear*thoven."

"Pooh, there *is* no Ludwig van Bearthoven. You wrote that song yourself."

"I did?"

"That's right."

"Oh, so *that's* where I heard it," he said.

But anyway, that brings us to what we're going to discuss here—enjoying life and being Special. Everyone *is* Special, you know.

"It is hard to be brave," said Piglet, sniffing slightly, "when you're only a Very Small Animal."

Rabbit, who had begun to write very busily, looked up and said:

"It is because you are a very small animal that you will be Useful in the adventure before us."

Piglet was so excited at the idea of being Useful that he forgot to be frightened any more, and when Rabbit went on to say that Kangas were only Fierce during the winter months, being at other times of an Affectionate Disposition, he could hardly sit still, he was so eager to begin being useful at once.

"What about me?" said Pooh sadly. "I suppose *I* shan't be useful?"

"Never mind, Pooh," said Piglet comfortingly. "Another time perhaps."

"Without Pooh," said Rabbit solemnly as he sharpened his pencil, "the adventure would be impossible."

"Oh!" said Piglet, and tried not to look disappointed. But Pooh went into a corner of the room and said proudly to himself, "Impossible without Me! *That* sort of Bear."

No matter how Useful we may be, sometimes it takes us a while to recognize our own value. This can be illustrated by the Chinese story of *The Stonecutter:*

There was once a stonecutter, who was dissatisfied with himself and with his position in life.

One day, he passed a wealthy merchant's house, and through the open gateway, saw many fine possessions and important visitors. "How powerful that merchant must be!" thought the stonecutter. He became very envious, and wished that he could be like the merchant. Then he would no longer have to live the life of a mere stonecutter.

To his great surprise, he suddenly became the merchant, enjoying more luxuries and power than he had ever dreamed of, envied and detested by those less wealthy than himself. But soon a high official passed by, carried in a sedan chair, accompanied by attendants, and escorted by soldiers beating gongs. Everyone, no matter how wealthy, had to bow low before the procession. "How powerful that official is!" he thought. "I wish that *I* could be a high official!"

Then he became the high official, carried everywhere in his embroidered sedan chair, feared and hated by the people all around, who had to bow down before him as he passed. It was a hot summer day, and the official felt very uncomfortable in the sticky sedan chair. He looked up at the sun. It shone proudly in the sky, unaffected by his presence. "How powerful the sun is!" he thought. "I wish that *I* could be the sun!"

Then he became the sun, shining fiercely down on everyone, scorching the fields, cursed by the farmers and laborers. But a huge black cloud moved between him and the earth, so that his light could no longer shine on everything below. "How powerful that storm cloud is!" he thought. "I wish that *I* could be a cloud!"

Then he became the cloud, flooding the fields and villages, shouted at by everyone. But soon he found that he was being pushed away by some great force, and realized that it was the wind. "How powerful it is!" he thought. "I wish that *I* could be the wind!"

Then he became the wind, blowing tiles off the roofs of houses, uprooting trees, hated and feared by all below him. But after a while, he ran up against something that would not move, no matter how forcefully he blew against it—a huge, towering stone. "How powerful that stone is!" he thought. I wish that *I* could be a stone!"

Then he became the stone, more powerful than anything else on earth. But as he stood there, he heard the sound of a hammer pounding a chisel into the solid rock, and felt himself being changed. "What could be more powerful than I, the stone?" he thought. He looked down and saw far below him the figure of a stonecutter.

Ah, here's the mail. "Oh, look—something for you, Pooh."

"For *me?*" said Pooh.

"For Mister Pooh Bear."

"*Mister* Pooh Bear?"

"That's what it says."

"Mister ... Pooh ... Bear," said Pooh in an awed sort of voice. "What's it say?" he asked, climbing onto the writing table and looking over my shoulder.

"It's from Fincnley's. *Announcing our third annual shoe sale. All styles, all sizes.*' Pooh, you don't need this."

"What's that say at the bottom?" asked Pooh.

"'Free Coffee.' One more reason to stay away."

"Let me examine this more carefully," said Pooh, taking it over by the window.

In order to take control of our lives and ac-complish something of lasting value, sooner or later we need to learn to Believe. We don't need to shift our   sponsibilities onto the shoulders of some dei-fied Spiritual Superman, or sit around and wait for Fate to come knocking at the door. We simply need to believe in the power that's within us, and use

When we do that, and stop imitating others

and competing against them, things begin to work for us.

Let's take a couple of examples:

In 1927, a thirty-two-year-old man stood on the edge of the lake in Chicago's Lincoln Park, planning to drop beneath the dark waters and drown. His daughter had died, his company had gone bankrupt, his reputation had been ruined, and he was becoming an alcoholic. Looking into the lake, he asked himself what one small man in his position could possibly do. Then an answer came to him: he was now free to take risks, to initiate action on his own, and, by doing so, to help other people. He returned home and committed himself to the work that he believed the universe wanted him to do, instead of what he had been *taught* to do. He watched the laws of the natural world and altered his own living patterns accordingly, eventually changing his life completely. Those laws were to inspire and support him in his greatest achievements. But without his believing and taking a chance, his contributions to humanity would never have been made, and no one would have come to respect the name of Buckminster Fuller.

In 1854, a boy was withdrawn from school in Port Huron, Michigan, for "causing trouble." He had been there for three months. That was to be the only formal education of his life. He later worked as a laboratory assistant. The job ended when he blew up the laboratory. His employer picked him up and threw him out into the dust, saying that he would never amount to anything. But he had a plan, and he wasn't going to let a little problem or two stop him. He wanted to learn the mechanical applications of natural laws. He eventually became the foremost inventor in American history, with over thirteen hundred domestic and foreign patents registered in his name, a name synonymous with problem-solving genius, the name of Thomas Edison.

The play-it-safe pessimists of the world never accomplish much of anything, because they don't look clearly and objectively at situations, they don't recognize or believe in their own abilities, and they won't stretch those abilities to overcome even the smallest amount of risk. For example, when Roo fell into the stream during the famous Expedition to find the North Pole, what did Dismal Eeyore do about it? Long after Roo had been carried away by the current, Eeyore halfheartedly hung his tail over the water so that Roo could grab hold of it and pull himself out—or, more accurately, so that Eeyore would get credit for having tried something. Of course, he didn't really expect it to do any good, and of course it didn't.

Who was going to rescue Roo? Panicky Piglet was jumping up and down and making noises. Ineffective Owl was instructing Roo to keep his head above water. Concerned Kanga was asking if he was all right. Captain Rabbit was calling out commands. . . . But Positive Pooh was looking at the situation, seeing what he could do about it, and trying something:

Two pools below Roo he was standing with a long pole in his paws, and Kanga came up and took one end of it, and between them they held it across the lower part of the pool; and Roo, still bubbling proudly, "Look at me swimming," drifted up against it, and climbed out.

"Did you see me swimming?" squeaked Roo excitedly, while Kanga scolded him and rubbed him down. "Pooh, did you see me swimming? That's called swimming, what I was doing. Rabbit, did you see what I was doing? Swimming. Hallo, Piglet! I say, Piglet! What do you think I was doing! Swimming! Christopher Robin, did you see me——"

But Christopher Robin wasn't listening. He was looking at Pooh.

"Pooh," he said, "where did you find that pole?"

Pooh looked at the pole in his hands.

"I just found it," he said. "I thought it ought to be useful. I just picked it up."

"Pooh," said Christopher Robin solemnly, "the Expedition is over. You have found the North Pole!"

As Pooh found out with the North Pole, once we see what the situation is and what we can do about it, we need to utilize everything we find along the way in order to accomplish whatever is required. More often than not, the things we need are there already, all we have to do is make use of them.

For example, when Piglet was Trapped by the Flood . . .

"It's a little Anxious," he said to himself, "to be a Very Small Animal Entirely Surrounded by Water. Christopher Robin and Pooh could escape by Climbing Trees, and Kanga could escape by Jump-

ing, and Rabbit could escape by Burrowing, and
Owl could escape by Flying, and Eeyore could escape by—by Making a Loud Noise Until Rescued,
and here am I, surrounded by water and I can't do
anything. . . ."

Then suddenly he remembered a story which Christopher Robin had told him about a man on a desert
island who had written something in a bottle and
thrown it in the sea; and Piglet thought that if he
wrote something in a bottle and threw it in the
water, perhaps somebody would come and rescue
him!

So he did.

And when Piglet's bottle came floating past
him, Pooh got the message. But then he had to go
see Christopher Robin in order to find out what it
said

So he corked up his biggest honey-jar, dropped

it into the water, and jumped in after it. And after a little experimenting with his boat,

he floated off to Christopher Robin's house, where the message was read and a Rescue planned. Then the two of them realized that they needed a larger boat. So Pooh got an idea:

And in an exciting Rescue, Piglet was saved by none other than the famous Pooh Bear, Discoverer of the North Pole.

"Say, Owl. Have you seen Pooh lately?"

"I rather thought I saw him putting something into the closet a little while ago," Owl replied. "I wasn't paying much attention to the matter, though."

"The closet? Well, I'll just take a look and——"

"What is it?" said Owl.

"Owl, *what* are all these boxes doing in here?"

"Boxes?" said Owl.

"And they're all full of . . . *shoes.*"

"Shoes?" said Owl.

"Look at this. Loafers, 8½ A. Sandals, 10 B. Oxfords, 12½ E . . ."

"All styles, all sizes," said Owl.

"Owl, I'm not quite sure, but I believe I Suspect something."

"It would appear that *Pooh* is the culprit," said Owl wisely.

"When you see him, tell him I want to talk with him, will you, Owl?"

"Absolutely."

The two Fearless Rescues just mentioned bring us to one of the most important terms of Taoism: *Tz'u,* which can be translated as "caring" or "compassion" and which is based upon the character for *heart.* In the sixty-seventh chapter of the *Tao Te Ching,* Lao-tse named it as his "first treasure," and then wrote, "From caring comes courage." We might add that from it also comes wisdom. It's rather significant, we think, that those who have no compassion have no wisdom. Knowledge, yes; cleverness, maybe; wisdom, no. A clever mind is not a heart. Knowledge doesn't really care. Wisdom does. We also consider it significant that *cor,* the Latin word for "heart," is the basis for the word *courage.* Piglet put it this way: "She isn't Clever, Kanga isn't, but she would be so anxious about Roo that she would do a Good Thing to Do without thinking about it." *Tz'u* not only saved Roo, discovered the

North Pole, and rescued Piglet; it also gave Piglet the courage to go get help for Pooh and Owl when Owl's house blew over.

Now Piglet, as we know, is a Very Small Animal, and not exactly the *Bravest* one at that, but when Owl's house fell down, Piglet discovered that he had more courage than he had *thought* he had.

"Hallo, Owl," said Pooh. "I hope we're not too late for——I mean, how are you, Owl? Piglet and I just came to see how you were, because it's Thursday."

"Sit down, Pooh, sit down, Piglet," said Owl kindly. "Make yourselves comfortable."

They thanked him, and made themselves as comfortable as they could.

"Because, you see, Owl," said Pooh, "we've been hurrying, so as to be in time for——so as to see you before we went away again."

Owl nodded solemnly.

"Correct me if I am wrong," he said, "but am I right in supposing that it is a very Blusterous day outside?"

"Very," said Piglet, who was quietly thawing his ears, and wishing that he was safely back in his own house.

"I thought so," said Owl. "It was on just such a blusterous day as this that my Uncle Robert, a portrait of whom you see upon the wall on your right, Piglet, while returning in the late forenoon from a——What's that?"

There was a loud cracking noise.

"Look out!" cried Pooh. "Mind the clock! Out of the way, Piglet! Piglet, I'm falling on you!"

"Help!" cried Piglet. . . .

"Pooh," said Piglet nervously.

"Yes?" said one of the chairs.

"Where are we?"

"I'm not quite sure," said the chair.

"Are we—are we in Owl's House?"

"I think so, because we were just going to have tea, and we hadn't had it."

"Oh!" said Piglet. "Well, did Owl *always* have a letter-box in his ceiling?"

But after the chair was pulled off of Pooh and he had taken a look around, he came up with a Plan. Owl would fly up to the letter-box with a piece of string, push the string through the wire in the basket, and fly down again. Then Piglet would hold onto one end of the string while Pooh and Owl pulled on the other end . . .

"And there Piglet is," said Owl. "If the string doesn't break."

"Supposing it does?" asked Piglet, wanting to know.

"Then we try another piece of string."

This was not very comforting to Piglet, because however many pieces of string they tried pulling him up with, it would always be the same him coming down; but still, it did seem the only thing to do. So with one last look back in his mind at all the happy hours he had spent in the Forest *not* being pulled up to the ceiling by a piece of string,

Piglet nodded bravely at Pooh and said that it was a Very Clever pup-pup-pup Clever pup-pup Plan.

And at last . . .

He squeezed and he squoze. and then with one last sqooze he was out. Happy and excited he turned round to squeak a last message to the prisoners.

"It's all right," he called through the letter-box. "Your tree is blown right over, Owl, and there's a branch across the door, but Christopher Robin and I can move it, and we'll bring a rope for Pooh, and I'll go and tell him now, and I can climb down quite easily, I mean it's dangerous but I can do it all right, and Christopher Robin and I will be back in about half-an-hour. Good-bye, Pooh!" And without waiting to hear Pooh's answering "Good-bye, and thank you, Piglet," he was off.

"Half-an-hour," said Owl, settling himself comfortably. "That will just give me time to finish that story I was telling you about my Uncle Robert—a portrait of whom you see underneath you. Now let me see, where was I? Oh, yes. It was on just such a blusterous day as this that my Uncle Robert——"

"Owl said you wanted to see me," said Pooh.
"All right, Pooh. Why the boxes of shoes in the closet?"
"I couldn't help myself," said Pooh.
"How's that?"

"Well, first there was the card for *Mister* Pooh Bear. Then when I got to the store, just for a look . . ."

"Yes?"

"The salesman was so *nice* to me. 'May I help you, Sir?' he said. He made me feel Important."

"Pooh, you didn't *need* those shoes," I said.

"I'll take them back," said Pooh.

"That's better."

"Lots of other people will be taking things back, too, I suppose."

"What?"

"I saw lots of people there buying things they didn't really need. All over the store."

"Quite likely," I said.

"I wasn't the only one," he said.

"Of course not, Pooh. A lot of people try to buy Happiness and Importance in the same sort of way. But *you* can be happy and important without doing that, you know."

"So can they," said Pooh.

Well, yes, that's true. So can anyone. Despite what Eeyore once said, when it comes to enjoying life and making use of who we are, all of us *can;* it's just that some *don't.*

Sitting contented by Walden Pond a few years ago, a Wise Observer wrote, "The mass of men lead lives of quiet desperation." The desperation may have been quiet *then*, we suppose. *Now*, it's deafening. But we don't have to be a part of it. We can stop our desperate clinging to hollow life-substitutes, and set ourselves free. When we make the first move, the process will begin.

And that brings us to the Tiddely-Pom Principle, which comes from a song by Pooh:

> *The more it snows*
> > *(Tiddely pom),*
> *The more it goes*
> > *(Tiddely pom),*
> *The more it goes*
> > *(Tiddely pom)*
> > *On snowing.*

It's sometimes referred to as the Snowball Effect, which can remind you of the time you pushed that little ball of snow along, and it got bigger and bigger until it got so big you couldn't stop it, and it rolled all the way down the hill and flattened the neighbor's car, and soon everyone was talking about the Huge Snowball that *you* let get completely out of control . . . and that may be why we prefer to think of it as the Tiddely-Pom Principle, instead.

Now the principle can work negatively or positively. It can promote cynicism as easily as it can encourage hope. It can build hardened criminals or courageous heroes, stupid vandals or brilliant creators. The important thing is to make it work for yourself and for the benefit of others, or face the Ugly Consequences.

Working with the Tiddely-Pom Principle, you use respect to build Respect. The more it snows, the more it goes:

> So Pooh hummed it to him, all the seven verses and Piglet said nothing, but just stood and glowed. Never before had anyone sung ho for Piglet (PIGLET) ho all by himself. When it was over, he wanted to ask for one of the verses over again, but didn't quite like to. It was the verse beginning "O gallant Piglet," and it seemed to him a very thoughtful way of beginning a piece of poetry.
>
> "Did I really do all that?" he said at last.
>
> "Well," said Pooh, "in poetry—in a piece of poetry—well, you *did* it, Piglet, because the poetry says you did. And that's how people know."
>
> "Oh!" said Piglet. "Because I—I thought I did blinch a little. Just at first. And it says, 'Did he blinch no no.' That's why."
>
> "You only blinched inside," said Pooh, "and that's the bravest way for a Very Small Animal not to blinch that there is."

Piglet sighed with happiness, and began to think about himself. He was BRAVE . . .

So that later, when Uninformed Eeyore discovered a new house for Owl to move into, and it turned out to be *Piglet's* . . .

"Just the house for Owl. Don't you think so, little Piglet?"

And then Piglet did a Noble Thing, and he did it in a sort of dream, while he was thinking of all the wonderful words Pooh had hummed about him.

"Yes, it's just the house for Owl," he said grandly. "And I hope he'll be very happy in it." And then he gulped twice, because he had been very happy in it himself.

"What do *you* think, Christopher Robin?" asked Eeyore a little anxiously, feeling that something wasn't quite right.

Christopher Robin had a question to ask first, and he was wondering how to ask it.

"Well," he said at last, "it's a very nice house, and if your own house is blown down, you *must* go somewhere else, mustn't you, Piglet? What would *you* do, if *your* house was blown down?"

Before Piglet could think, Pooh answered for him.

"He'd come and live with me," said Pooh, "wouldn't you, Piglet?"

Piglet squeezed his paw.

"Thank you, Pooh," he said, "I should love to."

Do you want to be really happy? You can begin by being appreciative of who you are and what you've got. Do you want to be really miserable? You can begin by being discontented. As Lao-tse wrote, "A tree as big around as you can reach starts with a small seed; a thousand-mile journey starts with one step." Wisdom, Happiness, and Courage are not waiting somewhere out beyond sight at the end of a straight line; they're part of a continuous cycle that begins right here. They're not only the ending, but the beginning as well. The more it snows, the more it goes, the more it goes on snowing.

Chuang-tse described it this way:

It is widely recognized that the courageous spirit of a single man can inspire to victory an army of thousands. If one concerned with ordinary gain can create such an effect, how much more will be produced by one who cares for greater things!

(Applause.) A Toast! To Gallant Piglet and Fearless Pooh—

Sing ho! for Piglet (PIGLET) ho!
Sing ho! for Piglet, ho!

and

> *Sing Ho! for a Bear!*
> *Sing Ho! for a Pooh!*
> *Sing Ho! for the life of a Bear!*

When they had all nearly eaten enough, Christopher Robin banged on the table with his spoon, and everybody stopped talking and was very silent, except Roo who was just finishing a loud attack of hiccups and trying to look as if it were one of Rabbit's relations.

"This party," said Christopher Robin, "is a party because of what someone did, and we all know who it was, and it's his party, because of what he did, and I've got a present for him and here it is." Then he felt about a little and whispered, "Where is it?"

While he was looking, Eeyore coughed in an impressive way and began to speak.

"Friends," he said, "including oddments, it is a great pleasure, or perhaps I had better say it has been a pleasure so far, to see you at my party. What I did was nothing. Any of you—except Rabbit and Owl and Kanga—would have done the same. Oh, and Pooh. My remarks do not, of course, apply to Piglet and Roo, because they are too small. Any of you would have done the same. But it just happened to be Me. It was not, I need hardly say, with an idea of getting what Christopher Robin is looking for now"—and he put his front leg to his mouth and said in a loud whisper, "Try under the table"—"that I did what I did—but because I feel that we should all do what we can to help. I feel that we should all——"

Yes, yes, yes. Well, anyway . . .

"Here it is!" cried Christopher Robin excitedly. "Pass it down to silly old Pooh. It's for Pooh."

"For Pooh?" said Eeyore.

Of course it's for Pooh. Because he's *that* sort of Bear.

"Just what makes *Pooh* so special, anyway?" said Eeyore indignantly.

"Well, Eeyore, if you read the next chapter, you may find out," I said.

"If we *must*," said Eeyore.

Nowhere and Nothing

"Where are we going?" said Pooh, hurrying after him, and wondering whether it was to be an Explore or a What-shall-I-do-about-you-know-what.

"Nowhere," said Christopher Robin.

So they began going there, and after they had walked a little way Christopher Robin said:

"What do you like doing best in the world, Pooh?"

(And of course, what Pooh liked doing best was going to Christopher Robin's house and eating, but since we've already quoted that, we don't think we need to quote it again.)

"I like that too," said Christopher Robin, "but what I like *doing* best is Nothing."

"How do you do Nothing?" asked Pooh, after he had wondered for a long time.

"Well, it's when people call out at you just as you're going off to do it, What are you going to do, Christopher Robin, and you say, Oh, nothing, and then you go and do it."

"Oh, I see," said Pooh.

"This is a nothing sort of thing that we're doing now."

"Oh, I see," said Pooh again.

"It means just going along, listening to all the things you can't hear, and not bothering."

Chuang-tse described it this way:

Consciousness wandered North to the land of the Dark Waters and climbed the Unnoticeable Slope, where he met Speechless Non-Doer. "I have three questions for you," Consciousness said. "First, what thoughts and efforts will lead us to understanding the Tao? Second, where must we go and what must we do to find peace in the Tao? Third, from what point must we start and which road must we follow in order to reach the Tao?" Speechless Non-Doer gave him no answer.

Consciousness traveled South to the land of the Bright Ocean and climbed the Mountain of Certainty, where he saw Impulsive Speech-Maker. He asked him the same questions. "Here are the answers," Impulsive Speech-Maker replied. But as soon as he started to speak, he became confused and forgot what he was talking about.

Consciousness returned to the palace and asked the Yellow Emperor, who told him, "To have no thought and put forth no effort is the first step towards understanding the Tao. To go nowhere and do nothing is the first step towards finding peace in the Tao. To start from no point and follow no road is the first step towards reaching the Tao."

What Chuang-tse, Christopher Robin, and Pooh are describing is the Great Secret, the key that unlocks the doors of wisdom, happiness, and truth. What is that magic, mysterious something? Nothing. To the Taoist, Nothing is *something*, and Something—at least the sort of thing that many consider to be important—is really nothing at all. Our explanation of this will attempt to give some sort of indication of what the Taoists call *T'ai Hsü*, the "Great Nothing."

We will begin with an illustration from the writings of Chuang-tse:

On his way back from the K'un-lun Mountains, the Yellow Emperor lost the dark pearl of Tao. He sent Knowledge to find it, but Knowledge was unable to understand it. He sent Distant Vision, but Distant Vision was unable to see it. He sent Eloquence, but Eloquence was unable to describe it.

Finally, he sent Empty Mind, and Empty Mind came back with the pearl.

When Eeyore lost his tail, who found it for him? Clever Rabbit? No. He was busy doing Clever Things. Scholarly Owl? No. He didn't recognize it when he saw it. Know-It-All Eeyore? No. He didn't even realize that it was missing until Pooh told him. And even then, it took a while to convince him that the tail was definitely Not There.

Then Pooh went off to find it. First, he stopped at Owl's house, and Owl told him in twenty-five

thousand monotonous words or more that the
Thing To Do would be to Issue a Reward, which
would involve writing out a ... (yawn) ... notice,
and putting it ... (YAWN) ... all over the ...
(umm). Oh, yes—where were we? All over the Forest. And then they went outside ...

And Pooh looked at the knocker and the notice
below it, and he looked at the bell-rope and the notice below it, and the more he looked at the bell-
rope, the more he felt that he had seen something
like it, somewhere else, sometime before.

"Handsome bell-rope, isn't it?" said Owl.

Pooh nodded.

"It reminds me of something," he said, "but I can't
think what. Where did you get it?"

"I just came across it in the Forest. It was hanging
over a bush, and I thought at first somebody lived
there, so I rang it, and nothing happened, and then
I rang it again very loudly, and it came off in my
hand, and as nobody seemed to want it, I took it
home, and——"

Aha. So Pooh returned the tail to Eeyore, and

after it had been put back in place, Eeyore felt much better.

For a while, anyway.

An Empty sort of mind is valuable for finding pearls and tails and things because it can see what's in front of it. An Overstuffed mind is unable to. While the Clear mind listens to a bird singing, the Stuffed-Full-of-Knowledge-and-Cleverness mind wonders what *kind* of bird is singing. The more Stuffed Up it is, the less it can hear through its own ears and see through its own eyes. Knowledge and Cleverness tend to concern themselves with the wrong sorts of things, and a mind confused by Knowledge, Cleverness, and Abstract Ideas tends to go chasing off after things that don't matter, or that don't even exist, instead of seeing, appreciating, and making use of what is right in front of it.

Let's consider Emptiness in general for a moment. What is it about a Taoist landscape painting that seems so refreshing to so many different kinds of people? The Emptiness, the space that's not filled in. What is it about fresh snow, clean air, pure water? Or good music? As Claude Debussy expressed it, "Music is the space between the notes."

"Wooh *Baby*! Oooaowee *BABY*! (Wanga wanga wanga.) Baby, don't *leave* me! (Wanga wanga crash bang!) Baby, don't *LEAVE* me!" (Click.) Like silence after noise, or cool, clear water on a hot, stuffy day, Emptiness cleans out the messy mind and charges up the batteries of spiritual energy.

Many people are afraid of Emptiness, however, because it reminds them of Loneliness. Everything has to be filled in, it seems—appointment books, hillsides, vacant lots—but when all the spaces are filled, the Loneliness *really* begins. Then the Groups are joined, the Classes are signed up for, and the Gift-to-Yourself items are bought. When the Loneliness starts creeping in the door, the Television Set is turned on to make it go away. But it doesn't go away. So some of *us* do instead, and after discarding the emptiness of the Big Congested Mess, we discover the fullness of Nothing.

One of our favorite examples of the value of Nothing is an incident in the life of the Japanese emperor Hirohito. Now, being emperor in one of the most frantically Confucianist countries in the world is not necessarily all that *relaxing.* From early morning until late at night, practically every minute of the emperor's time is filled in with meetings, audiences, tours, inspections, and who-knows-what. And through a day so tightly scheduled that it would make a stone wall seem open by comparison, the emperor must glide, like a great ship sailing in a steady breeze.

In the middle of a particularly busy day, the emperor was driven to a meeting hall for an appointment of some kind. But when he arrived, there was no one there. The emperor walked into the middle of the great hall, stood silently for a moment, then bowed to the empty space. He turned to his assistants, a large smile on his face. "We must schedule more appointments like this," he told them. "I haven't enjoyed myself so much in a long time."

In the forty-eighth chapter of the *Tao Te Ching,* Lao-tse wrote, "To attain knowledge, add things every day. To attain wisdom, remove things every day." Chuang-tse described the principle in his own humorous way:

"I am learning," Yen Hui said.

"How?" the Master asked.

"I forgot the rules of Righteousness and the levels of Benevolence," he replied.

"Good, but could be better," the Master said.

A few days later, Yen Hui remarked, "I am making progress."

"How?" the Master asked.

"I forgot the Rituals and the Music," he answered.

"Better, but not perfect," the Master said.

Some time later, Yen Hui told the Master, "Now I sit down and forget everything."

The Master looked up, startled. "What do you mean, you forget everything?" he quickly asked.

"I forget my body and senses, and leave all appearance and information behind," answered Yen Hui. "In the middle of Nothing, I join the Source of All Things."

The Master bowed. "You have transcended the limitations of time and knowledge. I am far behind you. You have found the Way!"

Gathering, analyzing, sorting, and storing information—these functions and more the mind can perform so automatically, skillfully, and effortlessly that it makes the most sophisticated computer look like a plastic toy by comparison. But it can do infinitely more. To use the mind as it's all too commonly used, on the kinds of things that it's usually used on, is about as inefficient and inappropriate as using a magic sword to open up a can of beans. The power of a clear mind is beyond description. But it can be attained by anyone who can appreciate and utilize the value of Nothing.

Let's say you get an idea—or, as Pooh would more accurately say, it gets you. Where did it come from? From this something, which came from *that* something? If you are able to trace it all the way back to its source, you will discover that it came from Nothing. And chances are, the greater the idea, the more directly it came from there. "A stroke of genius! Completely unheard of! A revolutionary new approach!" Practically everyone has had some sort of an idea like that sometime, most likely after a sound sleep when everything was so clear and filled with Nothing that an Idea suddenly appeared in it. But we don't have to fall asleep for a few hours for that to happen. We can be awake, instead—*completely* awake. The process is very natural.

It starts when we are children, helpless but aware of things, enjoying what is around us. Then we reach adolescence, still helpless but trying to at least *appear* independent. When we outgrow that stage, we become adults—self-sufficient individuals able and mature enough to help others as we have learned to help ourselves.

But the adult is not the highest stage of development. The end of the cycle is that of the independent, clear-minded, all-seeing Child. That is the level known as wisdom. When the *Tao Te Ching* and other wise books say things like, "Return to the beginning; become a child again," that's what they're referring to. Why do the en*light*ened seem filled with light and happiness, like children? Why do they sometimes even look and talk like children? Because they are. The wise are Children Who Know. Their minds have been emptied of the countless minute somethings of small learning, and filled with the wisdom of the Great Nothing, the Way of the Universe.

They walked on, thinking of This and That, and by-and-by they came to an enchanted place on the very top of the Forest called Galleons Lap, which is sixty-something trees in a circle; and Christopher Robin knew that it was enchanted because nobody had ever been able to count whether it was sixty-three or sixty-four, not even when he tied a piece of string round each tree after he had counted it. Being enchanted, its floor was not like the floor of the Forest, gorse and bracken and heather, but close-set grass, quiet and smooth and green. . . . Sitting there they could see the whole world spread out until it reached the sky, and whatever there was all the world over was with them in Galleons Lap.

There the Pooh books come to an end, in the Enchanted Place at the top of the Forest. We can go there at any time. It's not far away; it's not hard to find. Just take the path to Nothing, and go Nowhere until you reach it. Because the Enchanted Place is right where you are, and if you're Friendly With Bears, you can find it.

The Now of Pooh

In the morning sunshine, in the evening twilight, a small Bear travels through a Forest. Why did we follow him when we were so much younger? He is, after all, only a Bear of Little Brain. But is Brain all that important? Is it really Brain that takes us where we need to go? Or is it all too often Brain that sends us off in the wrong direction, following the echo of the wind in the treetops, which we *think* is real, rather than listening to the voice within us that tells us which way to turn?

A Brain can do all kinds of things, but the things that it can do are not the most important things. Abstract cleverness of mind only separates the thinker from the world of reality, and that world, the Forest of Real Life, is in a desperate condition now because of too many who think too much and care too little. In spite of what many minds have thought themselves into believing, that mistake cannot continue for much longer if everything is going to survive. The one chance we have to avoid certain disaster is to change our approach, and to learn to value wisdom and contentment. These are the things that are being searched for anyway, through Knowledge and Cleverness, but they do not come from Knowledge and Cleverness. They never have, and they never will. We can no longer afford to look so desperately hard for something in the wrong way and in the wrong place. If Knowledge and Cleverness are allowed to go on wrecking things, they will before much longer destroy all life on earth as we know it, and what little may temporarily survive will not be worth looking at, even if it would somehow be possible for us to do so.

The masters of life know the Way, for they listen to the voice within them, the voice of wisdom and simplicity, the voice that reasons beyond Cleverness and knows beyond Knowledge. That voice is not just the power and property of a few, but has been given to everyone. Those who pay attention to it are too often treated as exceptions to a rule, rather than as examples of the rule in operation, a rule that can apply to anyone who makes use of it.

Within each of us there is an Owl, a Rabbit, an Eeyore, and a Pooh. For too long, we have chosen the way of Owl and Rabbit. Now, like Eeyore, we complain about the results. But that accomplishes nothing. If we are smart, we will choose the way of Pooh. As if from far away, it calls to us with the voice of a child's mind. It may be hard to hear at times, but it is important just the same, because without it, we will never find our way through the Forest.

Backword

"Well, what do you think, Pooh?" I said.

"Think about what?" asked Pooh.

"The Tao of Pooh, of course."

"The *how* of Pooh?" asked Pooh.

"Do we have to go through *that* again?" I said.

"Go through *what* again?" asked Pooh.

"The Tao of Pooh," I said.

"What's the Tao of Pooh?"

"You know—the Uncarved Block, the Cottleston Pie Principle, the Pooh Way, *That* Sort of Bear, and all that."

"Oh," said Pooh.

"That's the Tao of Pooh," I said.

"Oh," said Pooh.

"How would *you* describe it?" I asked.

"Well . . . this just came to me," he said. "I'll
sing it to you."

"All right."

"Now, then . . . (er*hum*),"

To know the Way,
We go the Way;
We do the Way
The way we do
The things we do.
It's all there in front of you,
But if you try too hard to see it,
You'll only become Confused.

I am me,
And you are you,
As you can see;
But when you do
The things that you can do,
You will find the Way,
And the Way will follow you.

"That's what *I* think it is," he said.

"Perfect," I said. "But you know, don't you . .

"Know what?" said Pooh.

"It's the same thing."

"Oh," said Pooh. "So it is."

Also available in Mandarin Paperbacks

CHARLES MCKEOWN AND TERRY GILLIAM

The Adventures of Baron Munchausen

The adventures of Baron Munchausen, one of the most famous liars in history, were first set down in print over two hundred years ago and since then they have been retold and added to by storytellers around the world to the delight of frivolous adults and serious children everywhere.

This book tells the story of Terry Gilliam and Charles McKeown's exciting and hilarious new screenplay, which shows a company of actors in a besieged town – headed by Henry Salt Esq., the internationally famous actor manager and abetted by his daughter Sally. The play they perform retells the story of Baron Munchausen, but it is interrupted by an aged and outraged member of the audience who claims to be the Baron himself.

Only nine-year-old Sally will believe that he really is the Baron and so begins an exciting and enthralling series of adventures for them both, which starts with a daredevil wager against a murderous sultan and takes them to the moon and beyond.

True to the tradition of Terry Gilliam's *Time Bandits*, this story of the film offers a delightfully colourful adventure in time and space, a truly Munchausenesque extravaganza

MICHAEL MORPURGO

Why the Whales Came

Now a major film starring
Helen Mirren and Paul Scofield

"You keep away from the Birdman," warned Gracie's
father. "Keep well clear of him, you hear me now?"

But Gracie and her friend Daniel discover that the Birdman isn't mad or dangerous as everyone says. Yet he does
warn them to stay away from the abandoned Sampson
Island – he says it's cursed. And when the children are
stranded on Samson by fog, Gracie returns home to learn
of a tragic death Could the Birdman be right?

On the day the whale is found stranded on the beach,
the Birdman is forced to reveal his secret -- or the cycle
of disaster will begin all over again . .

SUE TOWNSEND

Rebuilding Coventry

"There are two things you should know about me immediately: the first is that I am beautiful, the second is that yesterday I killed a man called Gerald Fox. Both things were accidents."

So begins Coventry Dakin's tale. Forced to flee the law, Coventry deserts Grey Paths Council Estate, her prize-bore husband and two demanding children for the anonymity of London's Cardboard City.

Life as one of Britain's homeless, interspersed with forays into London's rich and influential society gatherings, teaches Coventry much about her country and herself. Her role in an imminent political scandal, offers her a chance to escape for ever . . .

Rebuilding Coventry is Sue Townsend's first work of fiction since her Adrian Mole books

"Entertaining, provocative and (naturally) utterly original." *BOOKS*

"The dialogue is splendidly witty and accurate, and the social observation sharp and imaginative. And the black, comical ending is typical Townsend."
SUNDAY EXPRESS

"Townsend writes with great charm and conviction."
THE SUNDAY TIMES

"This is satire in the best, Jonsonian tradition, with nothing and no one spared."
NEW STATESMAN AND SOCIETY

A Selected List of Humour Available from Mandarin

While every effort is made to keep prices low, it is sometimes necessary to increase prices at short notice. Mandarin Paperbacks reserves the right to show new retail prices on covers which may differ from those previously advertised in the text or elsewhere.

The prices shown below were correct at the time of going to press.

☐	7493 0159 7	**The Complete Fawlty Towers**	John Cleese & Connie Booth	£5.99
☐	7493 1436 2	**Class**	Jilly Cooper	£4.99
☐	7493 0849 4	**Angels Rush In**	Jilly Cooper	£5.99
☐	7493 0178 3	**The Common Years**	Jilly Cooper	£4.99
☐	7493 0252 6	**Turn Right at the Spotted Dog**	Jilly Cooper	£3.99
☐	7493 1116 9	**How to Survive Christmas**	Jilly Cooper	£4.99
☐	7493 1164 9	**Women and Superwomen**	Jilly Cooper	£3.99
☐	7493 1163 0	**Men and Supermen**	Jilly Cooper	£3.99
☐	7493 1165 7	**Mongrel Magic**	Jilly Cooper	£8.99
☐	7493 1355 2	**When Did You Last See Your Father?**	Jeremy Hardy	£5.99
☐	7493 1147 9	**Can I Come Down Now Dad?**	John Hegley	£3.99
☐	7493 3606 4	**Second from Last in the Sack Race**	David Nobbs	£4.99
☐	7493 0020 5	**Pratt of the Argus**	David Nobbs	£4.99
☐	7493 1015 4	**A Bit of a Do**	David Nobbs	£4.99
☐	7493 0138 4	**The Secret Diary of Adrian Mole Aged 13¾**	Sue Townsend	£3.99
☐	7493 0222 4	**The Growing Pains of Adrian Mole**	Sue Townsend	£3.99
☐	7493 0229 1	**True Confessions of Adrian Albert Mole**	Sue Townsend	£3.99
☐	7493 1120 7	**Adrian Mole from Minor to Major**	Sue Townsend	£4.99
☐	7493 1503 2	**Barmy**	Victoria Wood	£5.99
☐	7493 1314 5	**Up to You, Porky**	Victoria Wood	£5.99
☐	7493 0819 2	**Lucky Bag: The Victoria Wood Songbook**	Victoria Wood	£7.99

All these books are available at your bookshop or newsagent, or can be ordered direct from the address below. Just tick the titles you want and fill in the form below.

Cash Sales Department, PO Box 5, Rushden, Northants NN10 6YX.
Fax: 0933 410321 : Phone 0933 410511.

Please send cheque, payable to 'Reed Book Services Ltd.', or postal order for purchase price quoted and allow the following for postage and packing:

£1.00 for the first book, 50p for the second; **FREE POSTAGE AND PACKING FOR THREE BOOKS OR MORE PER ORDER.**

NAME (Block letters) ....

ADDRESS ....

....

☐ I enclose my remittance for ....

☐ I wish to pay by Access/Visa Card Number ☐☐☐☐☐☐☐☐☐☐☐☐☐☐☐☐

Expiry Date ☐☐☐☐

Signature ....

Please quote our reference: MAND